STAFF BURNOUT:
PREVENTION AND INTERVENTION
STRATEGIES FOR SOCIAL SERVICES

Doctoral Dissertation Research
A Mixed Methods Case Study

Submitted to the
Faculty of Argosy University, Phoenix, AZ
College of Business

In Partial Fulfillment of
the Requirements for the Degree of

Doctor of Education in Organizational Leadership

Dissertation Committee:

Randy Heinrich, D.M., Chair

Gerry Bedore, Ph.D., Member

Deborah Shearer, Ph.D., Member

Kate Noone, Ed. D., Program Chair

ABSTRACT

Staff burnout is a concern for researchers and

practitioners across organizations (Goethals & Sorenson,

2006; Rycraft, 1994; Schulz, Greenley, & Brown, 1995).

Employee burnout yields emotional exhaustion,

depersonalization, and a reduced sense of personal

accomplishment (Goodman & Boss, 2002; Maslach,

2003; Maslach & Leitner, 2008; Nurmi, Salmela-Aro, &

Naatanen, 2008; Siebert, 2005). The purpose of this

mixed methods explanatory case study was to explore

specific organizational coping strategies for preventing

staff burnout using the Pines and Aronson (1988) model

of organizational burnout prevention and intervention

strategies. Using surveys, interviews, and focus groups,

this study results indicated job burnout prevention and

intervention strategies include: (a) reducing staff to client

ratios, (b) promoting training opportunities, and (c)

improving work conditions. Future researchers should

replicate this study in alternative settings and address if

integrating the themes would reduce staff job burnout.

TABLE OF CONTENTS

TABLE OF TABLES

Table

TABLE OF APPENDICES

Appendix

CHAPTER ONE: THE PROBLEM

Burnout is one of the most significant

occupational hazards of the 21st century (Leiter &

Maslach, 2005) and is becoming an epidemic among

North American workers (Maslach & Leiter, 1997).

Social workers are one group, among many, identifying as

working in a helping profession, and for whom the

likelihood of staff burnout is great (Pines & Aronson,

1988). According to the 2000 U.S. Census (as cited in

Bureau of Labor Statistics, 2001), more than 840,000

people in the United States self-identified their occupation

as a social worker. Individuals employed in helping

professions usually work one-on-one with people or

groups and are more prone to burnout. Thus, suffering

from the primary burnout symptoms of emotional

exhaustion, depersonalization, and a feeling of reduced

personal accomplishment is common (Maslach, 2003).

Common reasons for burnout include; (a) increased

severity of client problems, (b) increases in paperwork,

(c) increased caseloads, (d) waiting lists for essential

services, (e) assignment to tasks not relevant to client treatment, (f) lack of oversight and available supervision, (g) decreased job security, (h) poor staffing levels, and (i) decreased levels of reimbursement for services (Licensed Social Workers in the United States, 2006). Issues of this type are important for organizational leaders because of the need to consistently attract and retain highly qualified employees in order to develop and maintain a high functioning organization (Goethals & Sorenson, 2006). Further, burnout is a noteworthy concern for social service organizational leadership because of the potential for staffing shortages (Licensed Social Workers in the United States, 2006).

Staff burnout has been studied in depth, as scholars offer related causes and development (Ducharme, Knudsen, & Roman, 2008; Elpers & Westhuis, 2008; Grant & Campbell, 2007; Pines & Aronson, 1988). Researchers have studied staff burnout across helping professions and recommended the following interventions; (a) professional retreats, (c) educational programs, (d) on-site professional resources

(Aycock & Boyle, 2008), (e) self-directed skills training

(Caston, 2009), (f) coworker support systems (Ducharme

et al., 2008), (g) organizational leadership supports

(Elpers & Westhuis, 2008), (h) personal recognition,

career promotion, and skill development opportunities

(Graber et al., 2007), (i) rehabilitative group sessions

(Hatinen, Kinnunen, Pekkonen, & Kalimo, 2007), (j)

prioritizing daily activities and eliminating activities that

are not essential (Leyba, 2009), (k) improving adult

workplace resilience through training (Liossis, Shochet,

Millear, & Biggs, 2009), (l) individual and group

psychotherapy sessions (Nurmi, Salmela-Aro,

Keskivaara, & Naatanen, 2008), (m) peer support groups

(Peterson, Bergstrom, Samuelsson, Asberg, & Nygren,

2008), (n) psychoanalytic and experiential group therapy

(Salmela-Aro, Naatanen, & Nurmi, 2004), (o) and couples

therapy training sessions (Schaer, Bodenmann, & Klink,

2008). Researchers have studied personal, professional,

and organizational burnout intervention strategies and

findings have varied (Borritz et al., 2006; Bowden, 1994; Gellis & Kim, 2004). There is limited research available on specific interventions implemented at the organizational level. Interventions that could be applied at organizations and merit further exploration include; (a) reducing staff-to-client ratios, (b) making downtime available during the workday, (c) limiting hours of stressful work, (d) increasing organizational flexibility, (e) promoting training opportunities, and (f) improving working conditions (Pines & Aronson).

Workplace stress is an environmental stress that can be instigated by events for people and must be dealt with to prevent burnout (Xanthakis, 2009). Emotional exhaustion, depersonalization, and feeling reduced personal accomplishment contribute to staff burnout (Maslach, 2003). The burnout process is often long and marked by extended periods of stress, emotional and physical exhaustion, and compassion fatigue (Aycock & Boyle, 2008). Staff working in the helping professions serves others, and research indicates that such professionals might require assistance to overcome work related stressors (Grosch & Olsen, 1994; Simendinger & Moore, 1985; Wilkerson, 2009).

Background of the Problem

The topic of employee burnout has received attention in recent years, and researchers have explored the connectedness of employee job satisfaction, retention rates, attrition trends, and quality of work (Grant & Campbell, 2007). Additionally, Harrington, Bean, Pintelio, and Mathews (2001) noted that employees with little intrinsic job satisfaction suffer from burnout quicker and be more likely to leave a position than employees with a higher level of job satisfaction. Managerial and leadership activities affect staff burnout, and scholars have noted that internal organizational factors are often more influential to burnout than external factors (Arches, 1991; Ducharme et al., 2008; Elpers & Westhuis, 2008; Schulz, Greenley, & Brown, 1995). Lewandowski (2003) explored the effect of employee frustration on burnout and found that powerlessness and frustration were the primary predictors of staff burnout and attrition.

The majority of studies on the topic of staff burnout relied on small representative samples (Ducharme et al., 2008). Siebert's (2005) national study about factors contributing to burnout included many of the same findings that were previously found in localized studies. Siebert indicated that burnout occurs in almost the same way, and for the same reasons, across the United States and possibly around the world.

The end result of an employee's work on a service or product can have a negative effect upon job satisfaction and a corresponding positive correlation with staff burnout rates (Graber et al., 2008). Graber et al. (2008) further noted that social services leaders' producing high-quality programs had lower rates of staff burnout and a positive relationship between internal quality control mechanisms and increases in staff morale. Moreover, staff morale has been linked to the employee characteristics of age, type of work conducted, years on the job, and work setting (Schwartz, Tiamiyu, & Dwyer, 2007). The work setting has an effect on staff burnout when staff members are not a good fit within the organization, or are not properly suited for the required tasks (Rycraft, 1994). Each of these factors could influence organizational and leadership issues pertaining to staff burnout and should be addressed through burnout research.

This study was reliant on Pines & Aronson's (2008) standardized instrument for measuring indicators of staff burnout known as the Burnout Measure (BM). This instrument has been employed across settings and is reliable at determining physical, emotional, and mental exhaustion, which is an indicator of staff burnout (Schaufeli, Maslach, & Marek, 1993). Staff was interviewed in a one-on-one and group setting to discuss the topic of burnout and staff's view of the efficacy of the proposed organizational-level interventions of (a) reducing staff-to-client ratios, (b) making downtime available during the workday, (c) limiting hours of stressful work, (d) increasing organizational flexibility,

(e) promoting training opportunities, (f) and improving

work conditions (Pines & Aronson). The research might

be helpful to researchers and practitioners leading staff in

the social services profession.

Problem Statement

Staff burnout is a concern for researchers and

practitioners in the organizational leadership field

(Goethals & Sorenson, 2006; Schulz et al., 1995; Rycraft,

1994). Staff burnout appears to be present within almost

every organization and in varying degrees and is a

concern for corporate leaders because it denigrates three

distinct areas of functioning; (a) employee morale and

productivity, (b) quality of services rendered or the

quality of products produced for clients, and (c)

profitability and efficiency of the organization (Borritz,

Rugulies, Bjorner, Villadsen, & Mikkelsen, 2006).

Employee burnout causes emotional exhaustion,

depersonalization, and the feeling of reduced personal

accomplishment, which has detrimental effects on

employees and organizations (Goodman & Boss, 2002; Maslach, 2003; Maslach & Leitner, 2008; Nurmi et al., 2008; Siebert, 2005). There has been little research conducted on the topic of burnout interventions about organizational coping strategies for preventing or alleviating burnout symptoms for staff in positions that have a high potential for burnout, such as the social services industry (Pines & Aronson, 1988; Potter, 1996). The organizational coping strategies that were explored as burnout preventions and interventions include; (a) reducing staff-to-client ratios, (b) making downtime available during the workday, (c) limiting hours of stressful work, (d) increasing organizational flexibility, (e) promoting training opportunities, and (f) and improving work conditions (Pines & Aronson). It is important to conduct a case study to identify organizational coping strategies that will act as staff burnout interventions and to confirm, dispute, or extend the effectiveness of implementing those burnout interventions at a social service agency responsible for providing rehabilitative mental health services.

Purpose of the Study

The purpose of this mixed methods case study was to explore specific organizational coping strategies for preventing burnout from the Pines and Aronson (1988) model of burnout intervention and prevention strategies at Youth Services (YS) located in the southwestern United States. YS provides community-based social services to youth and families, and employs more than 200 social service professionals. A mixed methods case study approach was employed and might uncover burnout within the organization (Yin, 2009). Further, the study could yield organizational interventions that might help alleviate and prevent staff burnout in other social services and behavioral health organizations. This study incorporated quantitative and qualitative methods through an anonymous, invitation-only, online survey to collect the data from the BM (Pines & Aronson, 2008), and from open-ended questions asked during in-person interviews.

Focus groups were conducted to gain insight into the dynamics of staff burnout. The study might corroborate, extend, or dispute the Pines and Aronson organizational coping strategies portion of the burnout intervention and prevention strategies model as well as further the body of knowledge related to organizational leadership and burnout in the social services.

Significance

Staff burnout appears to be present in most organizations to varying degrees. Corporate leaders are concerned about burnout and the related denigration of (a) employee morale and productivity, (b) the quality of services rendered or the quality of products produced for clients, and (c) the profitability and efficiency of the organization (Borritz et al., 2006). From an organizational leadership perspective, preventing and alleviating staff burnout through organizational-level methods is crucial (Angermeier, Dunford, Boss, & Boss, 2009). Employees appear to benefit from high levels of morale and satisfaction in the workplace, thus promoting efficiency and effectiveness. Happy employees might be employees that are more productive. Staff burnout counteracts employee satisfaction and high morale by creating a sense of helplessness, hopelessness, and despair in the workplace (Stalker, Mandell, Frensch, Harvey, & Wright, 2007).

Organizational staff should strive to deliver high-quality goods and services to remain competitive in the marketplace. If an organization's staff suffers from burnout, they might have difficulty maintaining a competitive advantage as the level of product quality and service delivery declines. This study could provide insight for understanding workplace-related stressors that lead to burnout, could involve exploring organizational-level coping strategies, and will focus on burnout prevention and intervention strategies that organizational leaders can explore. Organizational staff, leaders, and other stakeholders could benefit from this study because of the potentially positive benefit for the social services agency and its clients. The potentially positive benefit that workers and clients report was applied to the organizational leadership field of study, specifically to social services leadership.

Significance to Leadership

This case study provided data that can be used by organizational leaders for staff burnout intervention and prevention strategies. Ducharme et al. (2008) noted staff burnout within the social services is a serious concern for organizational leaders. Through the identification of staff burnout and implementing organizational prevention and intervention strategies, social services leaders might be able to understand staff burnout more fully. Understanding the significance of staff burnout in combination with appropriate intervention strategies might allow organizational leaders to be better equipped to address the issues of staff burnout and to provide more effective organizational-level prevention and intervention strategies. Finally, this research related the phenomenon of staff burnout with the organizational coping strategies presented by Pines and Aronson (1988) as part of a staff burnout intervention and prevention strategy. The

research will utilize a mixed methods case study design.

Nature of the Study

This case study incorporated mixed methods for

an explanatory, holistic single case design (Yin, 2009).

Many scholars have attempted to address the topic of staff

burnout across organizational settings and have arrived at

different conclusions about the efficacy of staff burnout

intervention and prevention methods (Maslach, 2003;

Maslach & Leiter, 1997; Potter, 1996; Simendinger &

Moore, 1985). This might be important as unresolved

stress in the workplace and unmitigated staff burnout

might lead to less productivity at work, decreased job

satisfaction, problems within one's personal life, and an

increase in rates of attrition. Maslow (as cited in

Shockley-Zalabak, 2009) addressed the importance of

meeting a hierarchy of needs, including: (a) physiological,

(b) safety and security, (c) love and social belonging, (d)

esteem and prestige, and (e) self-actualization. The

satisfaction someone might receive from work is part of

Maslow's second level (Shockley-Zalabak, 2009).

Workplace stress and burnout might interfere with an

individual's ability to maintain employment, thus

affecting the safety and security needs identified in the

second level. These basic needs, if not met, will remain a

primary consideration for the individual until satiated

(Maslow, 1948). Kant (as cited in Ciulla, 2003) posited

through the ideal of the categorical imperative that the

most essential aspect of life and humanity was to cultivate

and employ a respect and dignity for all people.

Considering the categorical imperative of respect for

everyone, including one's self, and the need for meeting

the basic needs of safety and security within Maslow's

second level, leaders might have a responsibility to

provide necessary organizational strategies to assist staff

in reducing and preventing workplace stress and burnout.

These organizational-level strategies might help staff

provide for their own personal safety and security needs

that Maslow deemed important and might help develop

the overarching ethical responsibility promoted by Kant.

Additional research from a leadership perspective appears

necessary to address strategies that can be applied at the

organizational level to help prevent and reduce staff

burnout. Pines and Aronson (1988) posited,

> Even organizations that are similar in size,
> structure, and function can have very different
> levels of worker burnout, depending on
> organizational flexibility, emphasis placed on the
> significance of the work, the degree of autonomy
> given to the staff, the variety of tasks involved in
> the work, the manageability of the workload, the
> availability of social support networks, and the
> comfort of the work environment. Different levels
> of burnout are reflected in such things as different
> rates of turnover, differences in staff morale, and
> differences in employee theft. (p. 181)

Employee burnout might have a direct influence on the

stress experienced by employees within the organization,

and identifying and reducing organizational stress might

play a key role in alleviating staff burnout.

Pines and Aronson's Organizational Stress Factors

This study specifically addressed the organizational stress factors presented by Pines and Aronson (1988):

> [The] ratio of the staff to clients, the availability of "time outs" in periods of stress, the amount of time spent in stressful situations, the severity of the problems presented by clients, organizational flexibility, training, positive work conditions, and work significance. (p. 188)

For the purpose of the study, the six burnout interventions are: (a) reducing staff-to-client ratios, (b) making downtime available during the workday, (c) limiting hours of stressful work, (d) increasing organizational flexibility, (e) promoting training opportunities, (f) and improving work conditions (Pines & Aronson, 1988). The six interventions took place within a social service organization.

Unit of Analysis

The unit of analysis for this study was a social service agency named YS whose staff provides one-on-one and small group behavioral health and rehabilitative mental health services for youth and adults in community,

home, and office settings. The agency operates in

Southern Nevada and serves approximately 300 clients

with a staff of 40 employees. The cultural system of

action for the project were personnel who provide direct

services as well as support staff within the agency.

Research questions (RQs) will guide the unit of analysis.

Research Questions

The following questions will guide the research

process:

RQ1: How prevalent is staff burnout within the
agency?

RQ2: How well do the six organizational
interventions of (a) reducing staff-to-client
ratios, (b) making downtime available
during the workday, (c) limiting hours of
stressful work, (d) increasing organizational
flexibility, (e) promoting training
opportunities, (f) and improving work
conditions presented by Pines and Aronson
(1988) characterize the prevention and
alleviation of staff burnout within the social
services agency?

Scope and Limitations

Findings from this research pertained to social services staff burnout and related burnout interventions. It was anticipated that the findings of this case study would reveal that staff within the organization suffer from burnout according to the BM and that organizational-level staff burnout intervention and prevention methods was effective at reducing and preventing staff burnout within the organization. Organizational burnout interventions might be important and was explored in detail in this study, but the BM would not emphasize or identify specific stress attributes or their weight relative to the measured level of staff burnout within the organization (Pines & Aronson, 1988). The burnout interventions that staff discussed were limited to organizational-level coping strategies.

The burnout interventions that were explored in this study were limited to organizational-level coping strategies and its six associated characteristics (Pines & Aronson, 1988). Other non-researched interventions might be useful and appropriate for preventing and alleviating staff burnout within the social services field. The scope of the project was narrowly focused on burnout in a youth social services agency and the exploration through discussion of the organizational burnout prevention and intervention strategies as posited by Pines and Aronson (1988) Research-specific definitions were used to guide the scope and limitations of the research.

Definition of Terms

For the purpose of this study, the following definitions guided the research:

Intervention: a procedure or action purposefully undertaken to actively reduce or eliminate an undesirable situation or circumstance (Deutsch, Coleman, & Marcus, 2006).

Prevention: this includes preventive measures that are based on an adequate diagnosis identifying risk factors and risk groups that theoretically and logically fit in with the problems and that are introduced and implemented in a proper way (Kompier, Cooper, & Guerts, 2000, p. 371).

Staff burnout: a phenomenon that occurs over a period of time and includes emotional exhaustion, depersonalization, and a feeling of reduced personal accomplishment (Maslach, 2003).

Summary

Staff burnout, particularly within the social service field, has been a topic widely debated by scholars (Ducharme et al., 2008; Elpers & Westhuis, 2008; Grant & Campbell, 2007; Pines & Aronson, 1988). Understanding the characteristics of staff burnout and related interventions may be an essential component of organizational leadership. The focus of this research was burnout within the social services. This study explored specific organizational-level coping strategies aimed at reducing and preventing staff burnout. Staff burnout within social services, and the importance of organizational-level coping strategies, is explored in the following literature review.

CHAPTER TWO: REVIEW OF THE LITERATURE

A review of literature on burnout, particularly related to burnout within the social services, revealed findings that varied regarding organizational leadership, makeup of the organization, and work being performed by members (Angermeier et al., 2009; Clark, 2009; Ducharme et al., 2008). The most common themes present throughout the review of literature detailed that (a) organizational supports are necessary to prevent and alleviate burnout, (b) social support and a team environment lessens burnout, (c) stress induced through organizational methods rather than through personal issues leads to burnout that is more deleterious for staff than other causes of burnout, (d) emotional exhaustion, stress, and a lack of coping mechanisms are at the core of burnout, and (e) organizational structure and leadership are much more pertinent to rates of burnout than are demographic factors (Arches, 1991; Borritz et al., 2006; Eastwood & Ecklund, 2008). The focus of this literature review is on exploring issues that lead to staff burnout, staff burnout related themes, and methods for reducing and alleviating staff burnout. This review specifically targets social services and staff, employee burnout, and staff working in helping professions.

Title Searches, Articles, Research Documents, and Journals

This research included scholarly journal articles, books, peer-reviewed journal articles, and other sources through the Argosy University online library, Argosy University interlibrary loan service, and Brescia University library with the following search terms: *social services, burnout, staff burnout, burnout prevention, organizational leadership, burnout intervention, attrition, and turnover*. This review contains information accessed from the following journal and book search engines: (a) EBSCO, (b) ProQuest, (c) Info Trac, Ebrary, and (d) Net Library. The search engines provided access to the following databases: (a) Academic Search Complete, (b)Business Source Premier, (c) Education Search Complete, (d) ERIC, (e)Master File Premier, (f)

PsycArticles, PsycExtra, (g) Psychology and Behavioral Sciences collection, (h) PsyInfo, and (i) SocIndex. The researcher utilized interlibrary loan services to obtain difficult-to-locate or rare books not available locally. Bibliographic and reference listings were utilized from scholarly sources, which added to the body of knowledge. The review included more than 50 articles that mentioned the need to study organizational burnout prevention strategies, but found no author that had conducted such research. Approximately 250 articles and books were gleaned during the research process. An overview of the history of social service work and burnout was necessary.

Historical Overview

The relationship between staff, the work that staff performs, and the interaction between staff and organizations has shifted drastically over the past century (Heifetz, 1994; Kotter & Cohen, 2002; Munro, 2008; Newton & Ford, 2006). Organizational leaders and staff have found it difficult to keep pace with the changes required within the organizational setting due to changes in the work environment, and staff members that have not been supported by the organization through the drastic changes to the work environment have experienced work-related symptoms not known in previous generations (Goethals & Sorenson, 2006; Schaufeli et al., 1993). A very specific set of historical factors that involved social, political, and personal changes led to work and organizational factors that inherently promoted burnout (Schaufeli et al.). Moreover, the following personal, social, and psychological changes to the American work contract have taken place over the past century, and had a drastic effect upon staff; (a) after World War II, there was a drastic shift from community-based social services provided by churches and neighbors to professional services provided by businesses and organizations, (b) social service work quickly became bureaucratized, isolated, credentialized, and highly professionalized, (c) government support for professional social services exponentially increased the demand for and accessibility of services, which increased the workload and the supply of trained social services professionals could not meet the demand, (d) the erosion of the traditional social fabric of America led to an increase in social problems, and the frequency, intensity, and duration of such problems also increased, (e) more recently, government cutbacks in funding for social services led to underfunded or eliminated programs that placed an additional burden upon the remaining programs, workers, and organizations, (f) American workers became increasingly alienated and disconnected from their social communities and placed a much higher emphasis upon gaining personal and life satisfaction from work, which resulted in increased expectations of work fulfillment and fewer resources to cope with workplace stressors, and (g) the professionalization and credentialing of social services staff led to extremely high expectations from clients and organizations, whereby professionals were unable to attain the expectations set forth by the organization, clients, and colleagues (Borritz et al., 2006; Paspuleti, Allen, Lambert, & Cluse-Tolar, 2009; Schaufeli et al.).

Each of these factors might have played a significant role

in contributing to the shift in the relationships between

staff, clients, and social services organizations.

History of Professional Social Services

The history of professional social services dates

back to the significant social inequities experienced

during the industrialization of America in the late 1800s

and was solidified after the Great Depression of 1929

(Brueggemann, 2006; Jansson, 2009; Kirst-Ashman &

Hull, 2009; Zastrow & Kirst-Ashman, 2010).

Brueggemann (2006) posited the following regarding

early social workers:

> At the turn of the 20th century, the field of social
> work was peopled by leaders of enormous vision
> and energy whose goal was nothing less than
> eradication of the overwhelming social problems
> of the day-grinding poverty, political corruption,
> abusive working conditions, exploited women and
> immigrants, and dangerous and unhealthy slums.
> These macro social workers wanted to create a
> wholesome, safe, and equitable social
> environment in which the American dream would
> be a reality not just for the rich, but for everyone.
> Jane Addams, Florence Kelly, Homer Folks,
> Graham Taylor, Harriet Tubman, Mary
> Simkhovitch, W.E.B. Du Bois, the Abbott sisters,
> Mary Parker Follett, Clara Barton, Lillian Wald,

and many other macro social work heroes displayed altruism and compassion, courage and character that we rarely see at the turn of the 21st century. The pioneering efforts of macro social workers such as these laid the groundwork for many of the social advances we continue to benefit from today. (p. xix)

The modern era of social services began in 1955 and continued until the late 1960s as professionalization and specialization of the field of work became the norm (Brueggemann, 2006; Jansson, 2009). Radical shifts occurred within the field of social services as a result of professionalization and specialization (Brueggemann; Jansson). Workers in the past and present experience the following while working in the social services; (a) significant increases in the demand for services, (b) work that is increasingly specialized and complex, (c) increased workloads, (d) more pronounced and significant issues presented by clients, and (e) deficient organizational and personal responses to workplace stressors due to major shifts in the social services workplace (Brueggemann; Jansson; Kirst-Ashman & Hull, 2009; Schaufeli et al., 1993; Zastrow & Kirst-Ashman, 2010). These shifts within the social services are present in the literature on

burnout.

Burnout

The term burnout originated during the mid-1970s

as a result of psychological research conducted by

Freudenberger and Maslach due to the increasing

frequency of specific problems encountered by social

services employees in the American workplace (Schaufeli

et al., 1993; Maslach & Leiter, 2008). Schaufeli et al.

(1993) noted the following regarding the historical

development and emergence of the concept of burnout:

> Burnout first emerged as a social problem, not as a
> scholarly construct. Thus, the initial conception of
> burnout was shaped by pragmatic rather than
> academic concerns. In this pioneering phase of
> conceptual development, the focus was on clinical
> descriptions of burnout. Later on, there was a
> second, empirical phase, in which the emphasis
> shifted to systematic research on burnout and in
> particular to the assessment of this phenomenon.
> Throughout these two phases there has been
> increasing theoretical development in which the
> concern has been to integrate the evolving notion
> of burnout with other conceptual frameworks. (p.
> 2)

Development of early burnout theory, while non-empirical, established the basic tenets that underpin burnout research. The relationship between the provider and the recipient is of the utmost importance and that providing such services can cause significant and sometimes harmful emotional stress and strain for the provider (Maslach, 2003; Schaufeli et al.). The early understanding of burnout as a theme and trend in the American workplace has led to scholarly interest for additional conceptualizations of staff burnout.

Early Burnout Conceptualization

After scholarly endeavors into burnout research began in the early 1980s, the primary focus was to develop a list of symptoms by which burnout could be identified. However, that proved to be a difficult task given the lack of a conceptual framework to build on (Maslach, 2003; Schaufeli et al., 1993). Initial burnout researchers had backgrounds in psychology and social psychology research. These researchers first identified a list of symptoms that described the burnout condition, including; (a) exhaustion, (b) boredom, (c) detachment,

(d) impatience, (e) cynicism, (f) omnipotence, (g)

paranoia, (h) disorientation, (i) denial of feelings, and (j)

psychosomatic manifestations (Freudenberger &

Richelson, 1980, as cited in Schaufeli et al.). The

symptoms were refined through additional research and

condensed into the most commonly used descriptive

definition of burnout:

> Burnout is a syndrome of emotional exhaustion,
> depersonalization, and reduced personal
> accomplishment that can occur among individuals
> who do "people work" of some kind. It is a
> response to the chronic emotional strain of dealing
> extensively with other human beings, particularly
> when they are troubled or having problems. Thus,
> it can be considered one type of job stress.
> Although it has some of the same deleterious
> effects as other stress responses, what is unique
> about burnout is that the stress arises from the
> *social* interaction between helper and recipient.
> (Maslach, 2003, p. 2) [italics in original]

The term burnout, reportedly originated with poverty

lawyers and others who described drug users. The term

was later adopted by Maslach in the 1970s and was

immediately recognized and understood by research

subjects during this early conceptualization phase

(Schaufeli et al.).

The burnout phenomenon is now studied globally

(Maslach, 2003; Peterson et al., 2008). Researchers have

made progress uncovering the issues surrounding burnout,

the specific causes of burnout, and strategies that can be

implemented to reduce, alleviate, and prevent burnout

(Aycock & Boyle, 2008; Clark, 2009; Drake & Yadama,

1996). Current findings might uncover additional

resources and supports that are appropriate for preventing

and alleviating burnout for staff in a variety of settings

and different cultures.

Current Findings

Recent literature indicates that burnout is a

significant problem in many organizational settings in the

United States and across the world (Peterson et al., 2008;

Yu, Lin, & Hsu, 2009). Many factors affect burnout in

the workplace and specific measures should be

implemented to negate the harmful influence burnout has

in the workplace (Glisson & Durick, 1988; Grant &

Campbell, 2007). Recent findings bearing further exploration include (a) organizational supports for the prevention and alleviation of burnout; (b) social supports and a team environment lessen burnout; (c) organizational stress is deleterious and leads to burnout faster than personal stress; (d) emotional exhaustion, stress, and a lack of coping mechanisms are core burnout attributes; and (e) organizational structure and leadership versus demographic factors yielding burnout (Arches, 1991; Borritz et al., 2006; Eastwood & Ecklund, 2008).

Organizational Supports

Organizational supports are practices or techniques that can be implemented within the organization to alleviate or prevent burnout (Bratton, Grint, & Nelson, 2005; Pines & Aronson, 1988). The term support specifically means, "contributing to a person's capacity" (Deutsch et al., 2006, p. 806), and when support is applied, "the recipient becomes stronger, or in some other way, more effective at whatever it is that he or she hopes to achieve. Support, then, is 'strength-building' assistance" (Deutsch et al., p. 806). Firm staff

that does not have organizational supports in place will

foster an environment that might promote burnout

(Grosch & Olsen, 1994; Maslach, 2003). Organizational

supports range from reducing staff workload and

implementing a rewards system (Leiter & Maslach, 2005)

to relaxation techniques and adjustments of personal work

attitude (Fishkin). The focus of this research is upon the

outcome and benefits of organizational supports within

the context of specific, targeted organizational supports

(Pines & Aronson).

Supports

Organizational supports, when implemented

within the structure of the organization, are effective at

reducing and preventing burnout as demonstrated through

educational supports, a supportive work environment, and

management interventions that target stress reduction

(Aycock & Boyle, 2008; Bowden, 1994). Bowden (1994)

noted that burnout prevention strategies implemented on

an individual basis are not as effective as the strategies

implemented and endorsed within the organization.

Bowden also noted that (a) modified work roles, (b)

reduced placement of blame for failure, and (c) fewer

idealistic expectations from the organization reduced staff

burnout. Organizational supports might frequently

require bolstering through educational supports for added

efficacy.

Education

Literature pertaining to education within the social

services indicates educational programs are organizational

supports reported to be effective at preventing and

alleviating staff burnout (Brilliant, 1986; Busch &

Hostetter, 2009; Caston, 2009; Doyle, Kelly, Clarke, &

Braynion, 2007). Brilliant (1986) noted that social work

education programs in colleges and universities, while not

an employer of social workers, have an organizational

responsibility to provide a high-quality social work

education for the organizations that will provide

employment for the benefit of the person receiving the

education, to prevent burnout, and to increase the overall

level of service the social service professional can provide for clients and staff. Moreover, Brilliant detailed the specific need for organizational improvement in the following areas of social work education programs; (a) better curriculum, (b) more fieldwork, (c) better supervision, (d) conflict suppression and resolutions skills training, and (e) improved policy training. Educational programs, both within social work education programs and in the workplace, might lead to additional learning opportunities.

Learning Opportunities

Learning opportunities sponsored by, and implemented within, an organization, is known as organizational learning (OL). OL is an essential organizational support to prevent and alleviate burnout (Busch & Hostetter, 2009; Caston, 2009; Doyle et al., 2007). OL opportunities must be available within an organization to prevent and reduce stress levels and to provide resources for professionals (Busch & Hostetter). OL opportunities may be structured or self-directed

(Caston, 2009) and should be provided through

curriculum and skills training group learning sessions

(Doyle et al.; Caston, 2009). Additionally, OL

psychosocial interventions conducted at the

organizational level, such as interventions conducted with

peers that target both psychological well-being and social

functioning in the workplace, were effective and

beneficial for organizations and staff (Busch & Hostetter;

Doyle et al.). OL opportunities might lead to improved

professional effectiveness and lower levels of stress for

staff.

Professional Effectiveness and Stress Reduction

Organizational supports to prevent and reduce

staff burnout must be tied directly to organizational

effectiveness and service effectiveness for the maximum

possible benefit for an organization, staff, and clients

(Glisson, 2002; Hemmelgarn, Glisson, & James, 2006).

> Intervention components represent "multiple
> levelers" that are "pulled" simultaneously to create
> a social context that supports organizational
> effectiveness... These overlapping and interrelated
> components provide examples of the types of

activities that can be included in the efforts to create organizational-based social contexts that contribute to effective mental health services. (p. 248)

Organizational supports that uphold both organizations and staff include participatory decision-making strategies, team-building exercises, continuous quality improvement and measurement, job redesign as necessary, development of networking relationships, acceptance of feedback, information assessment strategies, personal relationships with members, conflict regulation strategies, and regulation and stabilization of both the work environment and personal matters (Glisson, 2002). Appropriate organizational supports must be relevant and multifaceted in both scope and sequence to achieve the best possible outcome of stress reduction and burnout prevention and intervention (Glisson & Durick, 1988; Glisson et al., 2008).

Workplace Stress

One of the leading factors associated with staff burnout is workplace stress (Jaffe & Scott, 1984; Kompier et al., 2000; Maslach, 2003; Powell, 1993). Although

staff stress reduction techniques may be implemented by

individual staff members on a personal basis,

organizational supports are necessary to teach such

strategies because stress reduction methods are an integral

aspect of organizational supports to prevent and alleviate

burnout (Kompier et al.; Liossis, Shochet, Millear, &

Biggs, 2009). It is necessary for organizational leaders to

develop a specific approach for dealing with the work-

related stressors that lead to staff burnout. The following

methods have been suggested; (a) a stepwise and

systematic approach to stress identification, (b) a risk

analysis of each stressor risk group and risk factor, (c) a

package of specific intervention measures that fit with the

problems identified in the risk analysis, (d) an

intervention approach that fosters participation of both

employees and management, and (e) the sustained

commitment of top management to stress reduction

methods that will prevent and alleviate staff burnout

(Kompier et al.). Curricular-based programs and self-directed stress reduction techniques have been effective

for preventing staff burnout (Caston, 2009; Liossis et al.).

Stress reduction techniques are both a staff resource and a

therapeutic support, which might be important for

preventing staff burnout.

Resources and Therapeutic Supports

Organizational supports aimed at preventing burnout

involve access to resources provided by an organization

and poor access to relevant job resources are associated

with a significant increase in disengagement and burnout

(Peterson et al., 2008). Moreover, the relationship

between an employee and an organization acts as an

organizational support by increasing the investment of the

employee within the organization and the involvement of

the organization relative to the employee, thereby

reducing burnout via an organizational support resource

(Rycraft, 1994; Schaer, Bodenmann, & Klink, 2008). The

promotion of self-advocacy and at-work therapeutic

interventions are organizational supports that have been

effective at preventing and alleviating staff burnout,

preventing workplace stress, and improving overall functioning (Salmela-Aro et al., 2004; Schaufeli et al., 1993; Taris et al., 2003; Xanthakis, 2009; Yu et al., 2009). Group therapy sessions at work, implemented and encouraged by organizational leaders, were effective with both long and short-term benefits for reducing and preventing staff burnout (Salmela-Aro et al., 2004). Stress reduction and stress management skills training endorsed by an organization were instrumental in reducing and preventing staff burnout (Taris et al., 2003). Employer-sponsored employee assistance programs that promoted individual therapy and self-advocacy skills training have been shown to reduce and prevent burnout (Xanthakis, 2009; Yu et al., 2009). Many organizational supports suggested by researchers might also be social supports, and researchers might need to address whether the utilization of organizational supports should occur in combination with social supports and team supports for added efficacy.

Teams and Peer Supports

Peer supports in the workplace that assist in alleviating or preventing burnout consist of individual peer support, group peer support, colleague feedback, teams and teamwork, and an organizational style that allows the free flow of ideas and information between staff and management (Angermeier et al., 2009; Aycock & Boyle, 2008; Doyle et al., 2007). Teamwork increases skills, accountability, and commitment and is defined as "a small number of people with complementary skills who are committed to a common purpose, performance goals, and approach for which they hold themselves mutually accountable" (Katzenbach & Smith, 1993, p. 45).

Social Supports and Teams

Social supports and teamwork in the social services work environment are particularly important because most colleagues carry out the same type of work, are involved in and work to solve the same issues, and, when joined as a group, are able to gather information not typically accessible by one individual (Aycock & Boyle, 2008; Dyer, Dyer, & Dyer, 2007). Moreover, as was explored previously regarding organizational supports and psychosocial interventions, peer supports that include both psychological and social factors, along with peer groups and social support components, are highly effective at preventing and alleviating staff burnout (Doyle et al.). Schaufeli et al. (1993) detailed the description of social supports as follows:

> One of the most widely used definitions of social support is that of Cobb (1976, p. 300), who describes it as 'that piece of information which convinces people that others love them and care for them [emotional support], that others respect them and value them [affirmative support], and that they are part of a network of communication and mutual support [network support].'...Informative support is the willingness of other people to state opinions and give information. Instrumental support is the willingness of other people to give material aid. (p. 155)

Social supports present in the literature and that might be necessary within social services organizations involve emotional support, affirmative support, and network support (Glisson, 2008). Management and leadership should evaluate social supports and teamwork within the organization so that burnout can be prevented and alleviated. Schaufeli et al. (1993) arrived at the following recommendations regarding organizational supports; (a) every organization should have an organizational support system that matches staff and the organization optimally, (b) every support system should be maintained and supported by a matching work climate, (c) structure, support, and culture should be characterized by means of ethical criteria, and (d) ethical criteria should enable the prediction of which organizational factors might cause strain and burnout. Organizational supports might also include coworker supports.

Coworker Support Intervention

High levels of staff burnout correlated with low levels of social support in the workplace, and the intervention of coworker support demonstrated a significant increase in staff retention and reduced burnout (Ducharme et al., 2008; Hicks, 2008; Kao, 2009; Koeske & Koeske, 1989). Social supports and teamwork made organizational leadership more effective, thus indicating that leaders should encourage and promote a team environment in the workplace (Hicks, 2008; Kao). An organizational climate that fosters teamwork and social supports could benefit from reduced stress, and social supports have mitigated some of the burnout stressors of a heavy caseload in social services (Ducharme et al., 2008, Kao). Highly demanding clients and workloads contribute to stress and burnout, and if social supports and group work are lacking within an organization, burnout might occur quickly (Koeske & Koeske). Social and group supports within the organization might lead to a beneficial culture of positive support.

Culture of Positive Support

Social supports and teamwork should be at the core of an organization and integrated into every facet of the workplace to reduce staff burnout and promote positive emotional labor (Mancini & Lawson, 2009). If social supports are not in place, and if a team environment is not the norm, the lack of social support will lead to a breakdown in the team environment and will inevitably lead to significant stress, depressive symptoms, and burnout (Pedrini et al., 2009). Specific social supports that reduce and prevent burnout, contribute to positive emotional labor, and create a team environment include talking to others who are in a similar situation, task-related knowledge, sense of belonging within the organization and work group, self-confidence building exercises, group structure, relief of symptoms though social supports, and behavioral change through teamwork and social support (Peterson et al., 2008). Positive support might include the intervention of staff group therapy.

Group Therapy Support

Peterson et al. (2008) noted that specific social supports were effective at preventing and alleviating staff burnout and that group therapy in the workplace was effective across the burnout spectrum of emotional exhaustion, depersonalization, and reduced personal accomplishment (Grosch & Olsen, 1994; Salmela-Aro et al., 2004; Xanthakis, 2009). Regarding group therapy in the workplace as a social support, Salmela-Aro et al. stated:

> The results of the present study showed that both the psychotherapeutic interventions applied were effective in decreasing the level of severe burnout symptoms... [and] burnout decreased in the intervention groups compared to the control group. The results suggest that the relaxation and practice-based approach (experiential psychotherapy), as well as reflective discussion about the work situation (a psychoanalytic approach), were beneficial for individuals suffering from severe burnout symptoms. (p. 224)

The social support of therapy, specifically group therapy implemented at the organizational level, was effective at decreasing and preventing staff burnout (Grosch & Olsen; Xanthakis). Therapy for all levels of staff might provide effective management support.

Management Support

Social supports typically include management supports and structure whereby management and leadership provide ongoing social support and work to coordinate and facilitate teamwork efforts (Rycraft, 1994; Schaufeli et al., 1993; Schaufeli, Taris, & van Rhenen,

2007; Schulz, Greenley, & Brown, 1995; Stalker et al.,

2007; Van Hook & Rothenberg, 2009). Social supports

cannot exist in the workplace on their own without the

full support and investment of management (Rycraft;

Schulz et al.). Conversely, social supports that are not

fully supported by management and leadership will fail

and can undermine the benefits of social supports and

group work (Schaufeli et al., 1993, 2007). Stalker et al.

noted that when workers reported work exhaustion, yet

were supported through management-endorsed socials

supports and teams, the exhausted workers were less

likely to experience burnout than workers who were less

exhausted with fewer social supports. Moreover, workers

supported through management-endorsed social supports

and teamwork reported an increased level of life

satisfaction and decreased levels of burnout (Van Hook &

Rothenberg, 2009). Increased life satisfaction and

decreased levels of burnout might correlate with

decreased stress induced through organizational factors.

Stress Induced by Organizational Factors

Workplace stress is the leading cause of employee burnout (Borritz et al., 2006; Maslach, 2003). Personal characteristics might increase the likelihood of workplace stress (Grosch & Olsen, 1994); however, the most common culprit of stress experienced in the workplace is induced through organizational factors (Maslach, 2003). When employees and leaders understand the causes and implications of stress induced by an organization, then staff might be able to take those factors into consideration and mitigate them as much as possible (Doyle et al., 2007). This practice will act as a stress prevention measure, and organizational leaders might be able to make alterations to stress-inducing factors to reduce stress for staff (Angermeier et al., 2009).

Organizational Stress

Maslach and Leiter (1997) discussed in detail the factors for burnout induced by organizational factors and noted specifically that the causes of workplace stress are much more likely to arise from organizational stressors than from personal characteristics or individual stressors.

Organizational stressors specifically include work

overload, lack of job control, insufficient reward on the

job due to work overload, breakdown in the work

community and relationships, absence of fairness, and

conflicting values between management and employees

(Maslach & Leiter, 1997). The findings of Maslach and

Leiter were mirrored in the research conducted by Pines

and Aronson (1988). The organizational stressors of

work overload, lack of autonomy or job control, and lack

of reward contributed significantly to job stress and

increased rates of burnout were found in both studies.

Moreover, the methods for dealing with organizational

stress are an important consideration as organizational

and personal factors are essential for preventing and

alleviating burnout. Pines and Aronson stated:

> Obviously, some organizations are better than
> others on the dimensions of overload, power
> structure, and rewards. To the extent that an
> organization is structured in ways that increase
> such positive features as communication and
> autonomy, there will be a general reduction in
> burnout. At the same time, even the most

enlightened organizations cannot solve this problem for all of their employees. Individuals require sensible and useful coping strategies. (p. 111)

Stress Factors

Stress induced through organizational factors was described as factors related to the job setting (Maslach, 2003). The job setting is defined by the organization; therefore, job-setting stress factors might also be organizational stress factors. Job-related stress factors include: (a) work overload, (b) lack of control over the care provided or the job setting, (c) lack of or ineffectual peer or coworker supports, (d) ineffectual supervisory assistance or deficient leadership, and (e) burdensome organizational plans, policies, or procedures also known as bureaucracy (Maslach, 2003). Based upon these findings, organizational stress has the opportunity to permeate the work environment. If left unmitigated, these factors will lead to widespread burnout (Leiter & Maslach, 2005). Unmitigated stress factors might lead to organizational burnout.

Organizational Burnout

Various researchers discussed stress induced via specific yet individual organizational factors at length in the literature (Angermeier et al., 2009; Arches, 1991; Bowden, 1994). The topic of organizational burnout, or burnout at the organizational level, affects the whole organization from leadership to every employee, was discussed by Simendinger and Moore (1985) and touched upon by Arches (1991) and Maslach (2003) and described as bureaucracy. Simendinger and Moore further noted that organizational burnout can be measured by one of three factors; (a) whether an organization's leaders are burned out, (b) whether nonsupervisory employees are burned out, or (c) neither the leaders nor the employees are burned out but there is a breakdown or failure in a system such as communication or organizational goals. Organizational burnout will lead to increased workplace stress and burnout (Simendinger & Moore, 1985) and might be a function or inevitable by-product of bureaucracy (Arches; Bowden). More research should be conducted on the topic of bureaucracy given the obvious

importance of preventing staff burnout and the

bureaucratic structure of many large organizations

(Maslach, 2003; Pines & Aronson, 1988).

Bureaucracy

Stress induced by an organization on an employee

is more devastating than other forms of workplace

stressors (Angermeier et al., 2009). Bureaucracy is one of

the most common forms of workplace stress and reduces

job satisfaction for employees because bureaucracy

reduces autonomy, job control, and increases worker

frustration, which leads to stress and burnout (Arches,

1991). Moreover, bureaucracy leads to depersonalization

through increased regulation and agency control, which is

another precursor for employee burnout (Bowden, 1994).

Raquepaw and Miller (1989) and Schwartz, Tiamiyu, and

Dwyer (2007) noted that agency staff burned out more

often than therapists in private practice and that caseload

satisfaction correlated more with workers who were

overburdened and overworked than did the actual size of

the caseload. Bureaucracy of the agency might be considered an agency stressor.

Organizational Stressors

Staff stressors induced by the organization might occur through a combination of factors related to the agency, its makeup, and its mission (Bowden, 1994; Clark, 2009). While not all agency stressors may be eliminated for all staff, agency leaders can work to reduce or mitigate such stressors for the benefit of employees through organizational supports (Busch & Hostetter, 2009; Caston, 2009; Clark, 2009; Glisson, 2002). Organizational stressors are diverse and complex, require many types of interventions, and might include the following; (a) lack of control of work, (b) task ambiguity, (c) lack of employee evaluation and supervisor feedback, (d) absence of meaning or a sense of purposelessness of the work performed, (e) dissatisfaction with supervisors, (f) long work hours, (g) working in an agency setting, (h) working with extremely difficult client or with chronic illnesses, (i) clients who are burned out with the process,

(j) unrealistic expectations, (k) unresolved family of origin issues, (l) a need to be liked and admired, (m) inappropriate boundaries or over-involvement with clients, (n) a lack of meaningful workplace supports, and (o) the perception of having too many clients (Clark, 2009). Agency stressors might have specific implication for staff working in child welfare agencies.

Child Welfare Stressors

Organizational stress is present in many settings where the staff works with people (Maslach, 2003; Pines, 2002; Pines & Aronson, 1988). Stressors present within child welfare social service organizations are important (Brueggemann, 2006; Kirst-Ashman & Hull, 2009), with attrition rates due to burnout as high as 46% to 90% (Drake & Yadama, 1996). Staff stress induced by the organization involved; (a) depersonalization, (b) increased worker comfort, (c) increased role ambiguity and conflict, (d) increased values conflicts, (e) inadequate pay, (f) difficult working conditions, (g) lack of recognition, (h) chronic stress, and (i) overwork (Drake & Yadama).

Increases in workplace stress caused by organizational

factors are more likely to result in emotional exhaustion

and burnout than personal stressors (Doyle et al., 2007;

Drake & Yadama). Moreover, researchers have noted

that when organizational stressors are controlled through

agency interventions, staff members are less likely to

experience burnout and attrition (Bowden, 1994; Glisson,

2002). Child welfare agency stressors might affect the

climate of the agency and staff workload.

Effects of Climate and Workload

Organizational stress has a direct effect upon

employees' ability to function properly in the work setting

due to work climate (Gellis & Kim, 2004), and a poor

work climate has been linked to increased rates of

attrition due to organizational stressors (Glisson, 2002;

Glisson & Durick, 1988; Glisson et al., 2008). A poor

organizational climate leads to uncertainty in the

workplace, which, in turn, increases stress and is a

significant predictor of burnout (Grant & Campbell,

2007). Organizational supports might be necessary to

improve organizational climate, reduce stress, and prevent attrition.

Organizational stress can affect staff members through increased workload and overwork (Drake & Yadama, 1996; Koeske & Koeske, 1989). When organizational supports are low then organizational stress is high, and when a heavy workload is present the risk of burnout is exacerbated due to increased organizational stressors upon staff (Koeske & Koeske). Organizational and peer supports are necessary to counteract organizational stress induced by a heavy workload (Pedrini et al., 2009).

Paspuleti, Allen, Lambert, and Cluse-Tolar (2009) detailed how organizational stressors spillover into the personal life of staff and that a high level of life satisfaction for staff can be achieved through reduced organizational stressors. Moreover, Paspuleti et al. outlined the costliness of attrition when organizational stress is not mitigated effectively. Improved life satisfaction strategies presented in the literature proved to be influential and beneficial for employees at reducing

staff burnout, preventing stress, and alleviating depressive

symptoms through organizational stress reduction

strategies (Paspuleti et al., 2009; Pedrini et al., 2009).

The climate of the agency and staff workload might affect

the fit of staff within the agency.

Staff to Agency Fit

Organizational stress plays a significant role in

burnout when the staff perceives they are not a good fit

within the agency due to organizational style, work

investment, or supervision (Rycraft, 1994). The

relationship between the agency and the employees can

support staff or, conversely, might increase stress due to a

lack of support (Rycraft). Schaufeli et al. (2007) noted

that while workaholics are more prone to burnout in

general, workaholics who work in a supportive

environment with reduced organizational stress are less

likely to burn out than other groups. Workplace stress

induced by organizational factors notably increase the risk

of employee burnout, and stressors caused or contributed

to by the organization should be reduced or eliminated when possible (Maslach, 2003; Maslach & Leiter, 1997; Pines & Aronson, 1988). Stress is the leading cause of burnout, and leaders should be aware of how stress affects staff and how stress leads to emotional exhaustion, which is a major factor in burnout (Maslach, 2003; Pines & Aronson). Organizational implications of burnout are a common theme in the literature and should receive additional attention.

Organizational Implications of Burnout

Burnout is a syndrome that involves emotional exhaustion, depersonalization, and a sense of reduced personal accomplishment due to prolonged exposure to chronic emotional strain associated with doing people work (Leiter & Maslach 2005; Maslach, 2003; Maslach & Leiter, 1997; Pines & Aronson, 1988). Burnout affects both the organization and staff members (Pines & Aronson) and has multiple implications.

Dissatisfaction

Staff who experience burnout are less satisfied with the work they are doing and are more likely to perform poor quality work, become disillusioned, and have misperceptions about the work they are performing (Arches, 1991; Bowden, 1994). Staff members who are dissatisfied are less likely to participate in learning and advancement opportunities (Busch & Hostetter, 2009; Drake & Yadama, 1996). Staff members dissatisfied due to burnout are unlikely to take organizational commitments seriously, and detract from the organizational goals and mission (Glisson & Durick, 1988). Workers dissatisfied with the organization or the work they are performing due to burnout are more likely to leave the organization than satisfied workers are (Harrington et al., 2001). Staff dissatisfaction through burnout has been shown to lead to a lack of resiliency (Borritz et al., 2006).

Resiliency

Staff members suffering from burnout are less likely to possess resilient practices for recovering from stressful situations and to self-correct feelings of burnout (Clark, 2009; Eastwood & Ecklund, 2008). Training and education programs targeting personal resiliency and promoting resiliency attributes in agency staff are effective and essential for preventing issues related to burnout (Kompier et al., 2000; Liossis et al., 2009). Moreover, resilient staff members are more likely to promote positive attributes to other staff members and benefit the organization better than less resilient staff (Mancini & Lawson, 2009).

Attrition

Turnover is a problem for social service agencies because it causes instability for clients (Raqeupaw & Miller, 1989; Strolin-Goltzman, Kollar, & Trinkle, 2010). In one study, attrition rates for social service employees were reported to range between 23% and 60% (Strolin-Goltzman et al.). Staff burnout has been directly linked to turnover (Paspuleti et al., 2009; Raquepaw & Miller) and

is associated with increased agency costs and a reduction

in service efficacy (O'Donnell & Kirkner, 2009).

Agencies must work to reduce staff turnover through

providing supports, both personal and organizational, and

by reducing burnout via burnout prevention and

intervention methods (Glisson, 2002; Harrington et al.,

2001; O'Donnell & Kirkner). Attrition rates may be

linked to emotional exhaustion and symptoms of

depression.

Emotional Exhaustion and Depression

Staff members that experience burnout are more

likely to experience symptoms of depression and

emotional exhaustion due to work-related issues. Stress

and emotional exhaustion were a recurring theme in the

literature (Gellis & Kim, 2004; Ngai & Cheung, 2009;

Peterson et al., 2008). Symptoms of emotional

exhaustion and depression affect the (a) quality of life, (b)

absenteeism, (c) attrition, and (d) productivity of staff and

should be a significant concern for organizational leaders

(Gellis & Kim). The methods organizational leaders use to deal with emotional exhaustion and depression of staff members are directly related to the alleviation of such symptoms and the associated work-related issued discussed previously (Angermeier et al., 2009). Leaders should take the issues of emotional exhaustion and depression seriously and implement organizational structure and leadership strategies to combat such issues for the benefit of staff, clients, and the organization.

Organizational Structure and Leadership

The management structure and leadership in an organization play a significant role in staff burnout within organizations, and this theme is present throughout staff burnout literature (Angermeier et al., 2009; Eastwood & Ecklund, 2008). Angermeier Dunford, Boss, and Boss (2009) noted the following characteristics pertaining to management and leadership within social services; (a) some of the problems with staff management are rooted within the organizational structure and cannot be attributed to staff, (b) the most difficult to solve problems with staff are rooted in the organization rather than being clinical or financial, and (c) staff who were involved in a participative leadership environment demonstrated 79% lower burnout and 61% lower attrition than staff under authoritarian leadership styles. Moreover, an organization with a bureaucratic leadership structure will reduce overall job satisfaction and promote burnout (Angermeier et al.; Arches, 1991; Lewandowski, 2003). Given the importance of organizational leadership across various settings, a description of leadership is necessary.

Specifics of Organizational Leadership

Organizational leadership is a broad topic used to describe the act of leading and was defined in various ways (Northouse, 2007). Yukl (2002, as cited in Bratton et al., 2005) defined leadership as "the process of influencing others to understand and agree about what needs to be done and how it can be done effectively, and the process of facilitating individual and collective efforts to accomplish the shared objectives" (p. 6). Daft (2008) described leadership as "an influence relationship among leaders and followers who intend real changes and outcomes that reflect their shared purposes" (p. 4). The definition of leadership has and will continue to shift as the firms and staff change and evolve in the global workplace and shifting economy (Ciulla, 2003; Goethals & Sorenson, 2006). Northouse (2007) posited that leadership is a concept with many different meanings that vary depending upon the organizational climate, structure, and workforce. Moreover, Northouse listed the following regarding the concepts surrounding the components of leadership:

> Despite the multitude of ways in which leadership has been conceptualized, the following components can be identified as central to the phenomenon: (a) Leadership is a process, (b) leadership involves influence, (c) leadership occurs in a group context, and (d) leadership involves goal attainment. (p. 3)

This understanding of the concept and components of organizational leadership and structure might guide leadership in the social services.

Organizational Leadership and Structure

Researchers have identified that organizational leadership and organizational structure in the social services field are an important consideration for reducing staff burnout (Angermeier et al., 2009; Arches, 1991; Eastwood & Ecklund, 2008; Glisson & Durick, 1988; Leiter & Maslach, 2005; Lewandowski, 2003; Maslach, 2003; Maslach & Leiter, 1997; Pines & Aronson, 1988). Given the importance of organizational leadership and the role it plays within organizations, with staff, and in preventing and alleviating burnout symptoms, the concepts of social work leadership should be explored. Rank and Hutchison (2000) posited that five key elements must be present in effective organizational leadership within social services. The five elements are; (a) pro-action, (b) values and ethics, (c) empowerment, (d) vision, and (e) communication. Rank and Hutchison also derived nine leadership skills that are essential for social services organizational leaders. The nine skills were listed in order of importance from most important to least important in the following way, (a) community development, (b) communication and interpersonal skills, (c) analytic, (d) technological, (e) political, (f) visioning, (g) ethical reasoning, (h) risk taking, and (i) cultural competency and diversity. Based upon the five elements of leadership and the nine skills that are reportedly required for effective leadership, Rank and Hutchison defined leadership as follows: "Leadership is a process of advocacy and planning whereby an individual practices ethical and humanistic behavior to motivate others (clients and colleagues) to achieve common goals articulated by a shared vision" (p. 499). Rank and Hutchison went on to develop the following definition of social work leadership: "Social work leadership is the communication of vision, guided by the NASW [National Association of Social Workers] Code of Ethics, to create proactive processes that empower individuals, families, groups, organizations, and communities" (p. 499). Rank and Hutchison compiled each of the above-listed concepts and detailed the mission for social work organizational leaders as follows: "Articulate a vision to create processes of political advocacy in order to effect social reconstruction on behalf of those, who for various reasons, cannot participate in the economic prosperity of the global economy" (p. 500). According to the research on organizational leadership and structure, organizational interventions might be important for reducing and preventing burnout.

Organizational Interventions

Organizational leadership and management structures within social services organizations must have organization-wide interventions to prevent and alleviate staff burnout built into the management and leadership structure. To rely solely upon individual or personal burnout prevention strategies might not be sufficient (Bowden, 1994; Brilliant, 1986). Organizational strategies to support social services staff should include interventions that incorporate the organizational culture, climate, and structure. As Glisson (2002) noted, the organizational climate and structure are the only specific variables associated with higher rates of attrition. Elpers and Westhuis (2008) stated that staff burnout increases when the leadership style staff receives differs from the leadership style the staff expects to receive within the organization, that is, when there are incongruities between actual leadership and the desired or perceived leadership. Staff burnout prevention and intervention strategies within the organization must incorporate organizational leadership and management tactics as a core tenet of burnout amelioration (Eastwood & Ecklund, 2008). Organizational interventions might need to be based upon organizational factors of leadership.

Organizational Factors of Leadership

Organizational characteristics of leadership are the best predictors of staff job satisfaction and commitment to the organization, thus resulting in decreased burnout and lower rates of attrition (Glisson & Durick, 1988; Lewandowski, 2008). Lewandowski (2008) noted the following regarding the effect that organizational structure and leadership have upon staff interaction with

the work environment and levels of burnout:

> Organizational factors identified as contributing to
> burnout include multiple sponsorship of social
> work agencies, increased regulation, role conflict,
> downsizing, and role ambiguity...Role conflict and
> ambiguity, that is, lack of clarity as to what is
> expected, appropriate, or effective behavior, may
> be brought about by lack of communication about
> job expectation and roles, conflict with coworkers
> or supervisors...differences between organizational
> policy and expectations and individual
> expectations of fairness and equity, or value
> conflict with social work or personal values... To
> further emphasize the impact of the work
> environment, studies have shown that burnout
> may be caught from co-workers or supervisors on
> the job through negative communication. (p. 177)

Moreover, in the same study, Lewandowski (2008)

indicated that when workers experience significant

workplace stressors induced by organizational leadership

factors, workers will (a) experience significant feelings of

powerlessness and isolation, (b) be less likely to seek

assistance from leadership and management, and (c) be

significantly more likely to experience symptoms of

burnout.

Maslach and Leiter (1997) noted that failings within the organization, and ultimately organizational leadership and structure, were to blame for the majority of staff burnout. Feelings of burnout were reported to be contributed to by (a) being overloaded at work; (b) a lack of control over work-related tasks; (c) lack of reward; (d) an unreconciled and unmitigated breakdown in the work environment; (e) unfair treatment in the workplace by staff, managers, and leaders; and (f) values conflicts between work values and personal values. Leiter and Maslach (2005) reiterated the same concepts. They noted that (a) workload, (b) control, (c) reward, (d) community, (e) fairness, and (f) values were the most commonly cited aspects of the work environment contributing to staff burnout that were overlooked by organizational leadership strategies. Pines and Aronson (1988) arrived at similar findings regarding organizational factors that supported burnout, which included, (a) work overload, (b) a lack of autonomy of staff members in the workplace, and (c) a lack of reward and recognition of leadership for work performed. The style of leadership within the organization might play an important role in either contributing to or preventing staff burnout.

Leadership and Management Style

As mentioned previously, participative management can significantly decrease attrition and reduce and prevent burnout symptoms in the social services (Angermeier et al., 2009). Participative management is effective when the staff requires autonomy, such as in the social services setting, and when staff responds positively to being highly involved in decision-making processes (Northouse, 2007). Participative management is one of the four behavior styles present in the path-goal theory of leadership, and the four behavior styles are, (a) directive, (b) supportive, (c) participative, and (d) achievement oriented (Bratton et al., 2005). Moreover, the path-goal theory of leadership includes a leadership structure that has inherent worker supports, worker autonomy through leadership practices, rewards systems, worker-leadership participation, and other items that have been recognized in the literature as lacking, yet essential, in most social services organizational settings (Bratton et al., 2005; Northouse, 2007). The four behaviors styles of the path-goal theory of leadership were explained as such:

> The directive style is used when the leader must communicate expectations, schedule work, and maintain performance standards. The leader uses the supportive style when she or he wants to express concern for followers and create a supportive climate. The participative style is utilized when the leader wants to share decision-making authority with followers. And the leader employs the achievement-oriented style in order to set challenging goals for followers, encourage high levels of performance, and show strong confidence in followers. (p. 168)

Participative management has the characteristics to foster positive emotional labor (Bratton et al., 2005; Northouse, 2007; Angermeier, 2009).

Positive Leadership and Labor

Facilitating positive emotional labor is an essential aspect of leadership within the social services that may reduce and prevent staff burnout (Mancini & Lawson, 2009; Newman, Guy, & Mastracci, 2009; Stalker et al.,

2007). Emotional labor was described in the following

way:

> Emotions have been increasingly recognized in the
> organizational behavior literature as having an
> integral role in the effective provision of services
> that require human interaction. Emotional labor is
> the work of expressing and regulating affect or
> feelings in the context of paid employment in
> order to conform to professional and
> organizational rules. (Mancini & Lawson, 2009,
> p. 5)

Emotional labor is an essential aspect of social service

work, and organizational leaders must ensure that

organizational supports are in place to make emotional

labor effective and sustainable (Mancini & Lawson;

Newman et al., 2009). Moreover, when organizational

supports are not in place, and when emotional labor is

common in the workplace, staff will suffer from increased

emotional exhaustion, burnout, and high rates of attrition

(Mancini & Lawson; Newman et al.; Stalker et al., 2007).

Suboptimal job configurations, ineffective workplace

climate, and unsupportive organizational climates and

cultures are the most detrimental to facilitating positive

emotional labor, and workplace supports through

organizational leadership are essential for promoting positive emotional labor (Mancini & Lawson).

Various staff burnout intervention and prevention strategies can be explored by individuals and firms, but few are as successful as strategies that target organizational structure and leadership (Leiter & Maslach, 2005; Maslach, 2003; Maslach & Leiter, 1997; Pines & Aronson, 1988). Understanding organizational and leadership concepts related to burnout intervention and prevention strategies, along with the specific characteristics of leadership, especially social services leadership, might assist organizations, leaders, and staff in preventing and alleviating burnout symptoms. Moreover, details of social service agencies should be explored.

Social Service Agency Burnout Tendencies

Staff burnout includes symptoms of emotional exhaustion, depersonalization, and a sense of reduced personal accomplishment due to prolonged exposure to chronic stress and the emotional strain associated with people work (Leiter & Maslach, 2005; Maslach, 2003;

Maslach & Leiter, 1997; Pines & Aronson, 1988). Stress

in the social services was reported in the literature to

positively correlate with burnout in the social service

agency, and researchers noted that work-related stress was

the most common predictor of burnout (Coffey, Dugdill,

& Tattersall, 2004, 2009; Huxley et al., 2005; Munn-

Giddings, Hart, & Ramon, 2005; Sandmark & Renstig,

2010; Storey & Billingham, 2001). Moreover,

researchers who explored the social service agency

burnout tendencies of staff revealed the following

problems associated with agencies: (a) managed care

constraints, (b) increased budget cuts, (c) excessive

caseloads, (d) lack of resources, (e) organizational

restructuring, (f) inadequate management, (g) poor job

security, (h) lack of agency policies and procedures, (i)

role ambiguity, (j) lack of interdepartmental cooperation,

(k) job and workplace mismatch, (l) staff recruitment and

retention deficits, (m) distrust of management, (n)

excessive administrative duties placed upon staff, and (o)

clients' mistreatment of staff (Coffey et al., 2004, 2009;

Huxley et al., 2005; Lee, Cho, Kissinger, & Ogle, 2010;

Munn-Giddings et al.; Sandmark & Renstig, 2010; Storey

& Billingham, 2001). Lee et al. (2010) noted the

following deleterious effects of agency stressors: (a)

exhaustion, (b) incompetence, (c) negative work

environment, (d) devaluing clients, and (e) deterioration

of personal life. The prevalence of stressors in the social

service agency, and the positive correlation between

workplace stressors, burnout, and the deleterious effects

of stress and burnout upon staff and clients, might

indicate a need for burnout interventions.

Burnout Interventions

Based upon the review of literature related to the

description of staff burnout that details the specific

symptoms of burnout as (a) emotional exhaustion, (b)

depersonalization, and (c) reduced personal

accomplishment, it was discovered that staff burnout

interventions vary widely across similar work and

organizational settings (Fishkin, 1994; Jaffe & Scott,

1984; Leiter & Maslach, 2005; Potter, 1996). This might

be due in part to the multifaceted approach to burnout interventions that include personal interventions, social supports, and organizational interventions (Leiter & Maslach; Maslach, 2003; Maslach & Leiter, 1997; Pines & Aronson, 1988). Moreover, Maslach (2003) detailed the importance of the three types of burnout interventions in deterring the advancement of the burnout syndrome as interventions might (a) reduce the emotional strains of people-work; (b) offset the negative, depersonalized views of people; and (c) boost the individual's sense of personal accomplishment and self-esteem. For the purposes of this research, the burnout interventions that were explored by staff helped identify methods for deterring the burnout syndrome though proposed interventions implemented (a) personally by individual staff members, (b) social supports utilized within and without the organization, and (c) targeted organizational interventions. Personal interventions might be essential as a burnout intervention.

Personal Interventions

Maslach (2003), Maslach and Leiter (1997), and Leiter and Maslach (2005) noted that working smarter rather than harder is an important personal burnout intervention. Working smarter was reported to involve (a) setting realistic goals for work, (b) doing the same job in different ways to break up monotony and routine, (c) breaking away for rest periods, and (d) taking work issues less personally (Maslach, 2003). Maslach and Leiter (1997) reported that (a) reducing work overload, (b) achieving control over tasks completed and the workplace, (c) gaining more personal rewards for work completed, and (d) taking individual initiative within the organizational framework are essential personal interventions that will work to alleviate or prevent staff burnout. While Leiter and Maslach (2005) discussed the same important interventions, they noted that personal interventions must follow a specific pattern of steps that will guide the burnout intervention and prevention process. The steps are (a) specifically defining the problem, (b) setting objectives for goal completion, (c) taking action to remedy the situation, and (d) tracking progress.

Personal interventions for preventing and alleviating burnout include curriculum programs aimed at skills training by teaching coping techniques through the use of worksheets, questionnaires, and directed feedback based upon the outcome of the personal measures included in the curriculum program (Caston, 2009; Fishkin, 1994; Jaffe & Scott, 1984; Potter, 1996; Powell, 1993). Skills training and curriculum programs that have incorporated a variety of personal interventions have been effective at preventing and alleviating staff burnout (Caston, 2009). Potter (1996) noted that the objectives of such curriculum programs include (a) the identification of thought patterns that can cause burnout, (b) ways to deal with negative thought patterns, and (c) an exploration of the relationship between thoughts and feelings. Personal burnout curriculum and training programs have also been reported to teach (a) self-relaxation techniques, (b) skills for becoming more assertive in the workplace, (c)

improving negotiating skills, (d) studying the specifics of

the job to ensure an appropriate workplace fit, (e) time

management strategies, (e) thought stopping and

visualization techniques, and (f) shaping new positive

workplace behaviors (Powell, 1993). The following

interventions should be implemented within curriculum

programs that target personal interventions:

> (A) Reduce the pressure or demands from the
> [work] environment; (b) modify negative, self-
> critical, self-defeating, or other mental patterns
> that tend to create or amplify threats or dangers;
> (c) cope actively and effectively with demands
> and situations that trigger the stress response,
> thereby turning it off and avoiding the buildup of
> tension; (d) create supportive intimate and work
> relationships; and (e) practice effective techniques
> of tension management to avoid the negative
> effects of buildup of disabling tension. (Jaffe &
> Scott, 1984, p. 10)

Moreover, Jaffe and Scott (1984) noted that the following

guidelines are necessary personal considerations

throughout the burnout intervention and prevention

change process: (a) make changes in small steps; (b)

change one thing at a time; (c) have clear, concrete,

specific goals; (d) be aware of how you are when you

begin; (e) offer self-rewards; (f) find a support network;

(g) expect failures and relapses; and (h) use positive

imagery and self-talk. Fishkin (1994) specifically

addressed the importance of personal relaxation

techniques for preventing burnout and mentioned that (a)

progressive relaxation, (b) breathing exercises, (c)

meditation, (d) systematic desensitization, and (e)

hypnosis can be taught through curriculum and self-

training programs.

Burnout interventions that targeted individual

skills training for staff were effective at reducing staff

burnout, and researchers noted the long-term benefits of

individual strengths-based skills training (Hatinen et al.,

2007; Liossis et al., 2009; Van Hook & Rothenberg,

2009). Maslach and Leiter (2008) and Van Hook and

Rothenberg (2009) noted that although individual

interventions are effective, organizational supports that

bolster individual interventions are crucial for added

intervention efficacy. Individual interventions that can

also be supported by the organization include (a) envisioning and carrying out the ideal role of staff, (b) weeding out unnecessary tasks, (c) communicating needs and other issues with supervisors, (d) managing the caseload appropriately, (e) developing a strong referral process for clients, and (f) offering classes that promote both individual and organizational objectives (Leyba, 2009).

Recent developments in individual staff burnout intervention and prevention measures have developed because of increased rates of attrition due to burnout and the corresponding response at the organizational level to prevent burnout through employee supports, particularly within human resources corporate function (Bohlander & Snell, 2007; Rycraft, 1994; Yu et al., 2009). Individual therapy sessions that targeted stress personal reduction methods, as well as couples therapy for partners to reduce at-home strife due to work-related burnout were highly effective at reducing and preventing burnout and alleviating burnout symptoms (Salmela-Aro et al., 2004;

Schaer et al., 2008; Xanthakis, 2009). Organizational

leaders who promoted employee assistance programs that

targeted personal self-efficacy reduced stress and staff

burnout (Yu et al., 2009). Individual burnout supports

should also include social supports within and outside the

organization.

Social Supports

Social supports to alleviate and prevent staff

burnout may be comprised of peers, colleagues,

coworkers, and friends and family, and the importance of

positive social supports has been underscored repeatedly

in the literature (Bowden, 1994; Eastwood & Ecklund,

2008; Grosch & Olsen, 1994; Maslach, 2003; Maslach &

Leiter, 2008; Pines & Aronson, 1988). Maslach (2003)

cited the following regarding social supports:

> Getting away from people is a common response
> when emotional overload [burnout] is high. The
> desire for peace and privacy is certainly
> understandable, and these needs can be satisfied in
> constructive ways. However, occasional solitude
> is not the same thing as frequent isolation. The
> drawback comes when getting away from others is
> overdone to the point where you cut yourself off
> from some valuable resources. Getting together

with people is just as important (if not more so)
than getting away from them. People can provide
many things that you cannot provide for
yourself—new information and insights, training
in new skills, recognition and feedback, emotional
support, advice, and help of various kinds. Some
of these things can be provided by a spouse or
close friend. But, in many cases, the people who
are best qualified to provide job-related help and
support are the people on the job—your coworkers. (pp. 182-183)

Social supports may come in the form of help, comfort,

insight, comparison, rewards, humor, escape, and group

work (Maslach, 2003). Pines and Aronson posited that

social support systems serve the following six

fundamental functions: (a) listening, (b) technical support,

(c) technical challenge, (d) emotional support, (e)

emotional challenge, and (f) social reality. Deficiencies

in social supports lead to divisiveness, poor

communication, alienation, and burnout (Leiter &

Maslach, 2005).

Social supports might also include group therapy

sessions and trainings that include coworkers, thus

resulting in a shared social experience (Salmela-Aro et al.,

2004; Schaer et al., 2008; Xanthakis, 2009). Shared

coworker social support in conjunction with therapy

intervention are reported to be equally important and

might not be as effective if used individually without the

coworker's social support (Van Hook & Rothenberg,

2009; Xanthakis, 2009). Social support received by staff

in the form of group stress management training has been

deemed highly effective, both long and short term, at

preventing and reducing staff stress and associated

burnout (Taris et al., 2003). Social supports might also

include organizational interventions.

Organizational Interventions

As the scope of staff burnout research widens, it

has become evident that interventions implemented at the

organizational level are essential for reducing and

preventing staff burnout and that organizational

interventions might be more effective at alleviating staff

burnout than personal interventions that employees

implement without organizational supports (Borritz et al.,

2006; Leiter & Maslach, 2005; Maslach, 2003; Maslach

& Leiter, 1997, 2008; Pines & Aronson, 1988). Maslach

(2003) cited the following when describing the

importance of organizational interventions aimed and

preventing and reducing staff burnout:

> There are several reasons why it is important to
> push for organizational changes, and not just
> personal ones. First, although individual coping
> techniques may be quicker and easier,
> improvements of the workplace may have a more
> pervasive and long-lasting impact on the rates of
> burnout. Teaching people how to cope with a
> stressful job is certainly helpful, but it may not be
> as effective as making the job less stressful to
> begin with. Second, organizational changes
> acknowledge the significance of the situation in
> burnout. This can counter the overwhelming (and
> sometimes erroneous) tendency to blame either
> oneself or one's recipients. Third, an
> organizational response to burnout constitutes
> recognition of it as a legitimate problem. For
> many years, the problem of burnout was either
> pooh-poohed or swept under the rug. It was not
> acceptable to talk about it or to request special
> considerations because of it. Once organizations
> recognize that burnout is a real and serious
> problem for them and their employees, then
> greater efforts may be made to deal effectively
> with it. (p. 196)

Maslach (2003) went on to suggest the following

organizational supports for alleviating staff burnout,

which included: (a) securing additional resources, (b)

improvements in the division of labor, (c) changing or

revising contact between clients and staff, (d) limiting job

spillover as much as possible, (e) allowing staff time off

work, and (f) seeking and receiving help from coworkers

and managers. Pines and Aronson (1988) noted similar

organizational strategies that include: (a) reducing staff–

client ratios, (b) making time-out available, (c) limiting

hours of stressful work, (d) increasing organizational

flexibility, (e) training, and (f) improving work

conditions. Additionally, for the organizational

approaches to be effective the methods must (a) start with

management, (b) become an organizational project, and

(c) connect with staff; further, the outcome must become

a corporate process (Maslach & Leiter, 1997).

The importance of organizational strategies in

combination with personal burnout prevention methods

has been underscored in the literature, and many of the

organizational strategies that might be effective at

alleviating burnout require staff participation and buy-in

(Bowden, 1994; Brilliant, 1986; Busch & Hostetter, 2009;

Caston, 2009). Eastwood and Ecklund (2008) stated the

following organizational interventions also require staff participation, (a) time given by the organization to consult with peers and supervisors through planned activities, (b) adequate and appropriate training that will foster a sense of efficacy and preparedness, (c) sufficient staffing levels to support all staff, (d) employer support and encouragement of appropriate self-care practices at work, (e) adequate time off with the ability to use such time off, and (f) corporate benefits programs that allow for burnout prevention measures, such as mental health and physical health programs. Organizational interventions that have limited application, that are not practical, or that cannot be utilized by staff might have little positive benefit for staff and the organization.

Just as the efficacy of organizational interventions depends upon the buy-in of staff, the participation of the organization with the intervention is equally important (Glisson, 2002; Hatinen et al., 2007; Hemmelgarn et al., 2006). Participatory management style and interventions that garner participation from both leaders and staff have

been highly effective (Hatinen et al.; Hemmelgarn et al.).
Some components of participatory organizational
interventions that have been shown to be effective at
alleviating staff burnout include (a) participatory
decision-making regarding corporate structure and
services, (b) team-building exercises, (c) job redesign to
alleviate barriers for clients and staff, (d) conflict
resolution skills training for staff, and (e) stabilization and
self-regulation of services and programs for clients and
staff sponsored by the organization (Glisson).

Summary

Burnout in the social services is caused by
prolonged exposure to stress and emotional strain in the
workplace due to the intensive nature of social service
work (Leiter & Maslach, 2005; Maslach, 2003; Pines &
Aronson, 1988). Staff burnout interventions are
necessary to prevent and alleviate staff burnout.
Additional research might be necessary to determine the
efficacy of staff burnout interventions implemented
within the organization. The methodology of the study is

an important consideration and is explored in the Chapter

Three.

CHAPTER THREE: METHODOLOGY

A mixed methods case study research design may be appropriate for exploring the efficacy of the organizational burnout prevention methods posited by Pines and Aronson (1988). The mixed methods case study design follows Yin's (2009) holistic, explanatory, single-case design, and "investigate[s] a contemporary phenomenon in depth and within its real-life context, especially when the boundaries between phenomenon and context are not clearly evident" (p. 18). Staff burnout within the social services has been described as a significant occupations hazard (Leiter & Maslach, 2005), and may be approaching epidemic proportions among North American workers, especially for workers in the social services (Maslach & Leiter, 1997, 2008; Pines & Aronson, 1988). Pines and Aronson identified burnout prevention methods that may be effective for reducing burnout in the social services, when applied within the organization.

A mixed methods, explanatory, single-case study design to "cope with the technically distinctive situation in which there will be many more variables of interest than data points, and…rely on multiple sources of evidence, with data needing to converge in a triangulation fashion" was employed (Yin, 2009, p. 18). The cultural system of action that was explored included staff within a social service agency in Southern Nevada. Using surveys, interviews, and focus groups, I assessed the degree of staff burnout, explored with staff Pines and Aronson's (1988) organizational burnout interventions, and reassessed for subsequent differences. In this chapter, the (a) study's questions, (b) propositions, (c) unit of analysis, (d) logic that links the data to the propositions, and (e) criteria for interpreting the findings are addressed (Yin, 2009).

The triangulation design of this mixed methods case study included the convergence model (Creswell & Clark, 2007). Triangulation involved using different sources and methods of information in order to increase the validity of a study (Thurmond, 2001). However,

according to Evers and van Staa (2009),

> Triangulation cannot increase validity in the sense
> of pursuing objective truth; instead, it adds to the
> investigator's depth and breadth of understanding.
> Triangulation is thus seen as a means of enhancing
> the completeness of the findings, rendering a more
> in-depth understanding (p. 750).

As such, I triangulated data from online staff

surveys, focus group, and individual staff interviews.

Triangulation of these data sources allowed for

exploratory and emergent interpretation of the evidence

and corroborating the same information (Yin, 2009).

According to Creswell and Clark (2007), in a mixed

method design, data are collected separately and the

different results are converged through contrasting of the

results during the interpretation. The qualitative data was

used to address a distinct research objective, and

expanded upon the quantitative findings, and vice versa.

A mixed method was employed, as this allowed for a

complementary approach to concurrently bring together

the differing strengths of the methods, and compensate for

their individual approach weaknesses (Creswell, 2009).

Triangulation assisted in leveraging multiple data sources

and allowed access to different subjects and methods

within a common system. The design of the mixed

methods case study follows.

Research Questions

The following questions guided the research:

RQ1: How prevalent is staff burnout within the agency?

RQ2: How well do the six organizational interventions of (a) reducing staff-to-client ratios, (b) making downtime available during the workday, (c) limiting hours of stressful work, (d) increasing organizational flexibility, (e) promoting training opportunities, (f) and improving work conditions presented by Pines and Aronson (1988) characterize prevention and alleviation of staff burnout within the social services agency?

Unit of Analysis

This study investigated the social service agency

named Youth Services (YS) [pseudonym] whose staff

provide therapy, and one-on-one and small group

behavioral health and rehabilitative mental health services

for youth and adults in the community, home, and office settings in a large metropolitan city. The agency staff operates in Southern Nevada and serves approximately 300 clients with 40 employees. The cultural system of action for the project included personnel that provide direct services as well as support staff within the agency. Research questions guided the unit of analysis. The unit of analysis was corroborated with logic linking data to the propositions. Pines and Aronson's (1988) organizational coping strategies provided the basis for identifying and understanding the intervention outcomes.

Logic Linking Data to the Propositions

Yin (2009) posited that a desirable technique for case study analysis is pattern-matching logic linking data to related propositions. Based upon the results of the BM assessment to explore the level of staff burnout, and the efficacy of Pines and Aronson's organizational burnout prevention strategies, the results of the data collected were evaluated for the purposes of measuring staff burnout and the propositions and alternative propositions related to burnout prevention and intervention strategies (Pines & Aronson, 1988). Subsequent findings were factored when assessing propositions and alternate propositions. Pines and Aronson's six organization burnout interventions include (a) reducing staff-to-client ratios, (b) making downtime available during the workday, (c) limiting hours of stressful work, (d) increasing organizational flexibility, (e) promoting training opportunities, (f) and improving work conditions. This study used the inputs from Pines and Aronson's (1988) study as basis of the propositions. Propositions include:

1. Reducing staff-to-client ratios should decrease staff burnout.

2. Making downtime available during the workday should decrease staff burnout.

3. Limiting hours of stressful work should decrease staff burnout.

4. Increasing organizational flexibility should decrease staff burnout.

5. Promoting training opportunities should decrease staff burnout.

6. Improving work conditions should decrease staff burnout.

Alternate propositions may identify themes not previously identified by Pines and Aronson (1988) and may include:

1. Proposed interventions may temporarily decrease staff burnout, may not decrease staff burnout, or may increase staff burnout.

2. Emergent themes to include alternate interventions to decrease staff burnout may develop. Examples of emergent themes to decrease staff burnout may include the efficacy of group work or project sharing, leveraging staff from different departments to assist with non-routine tasks, or weekly strategy sessions to discuss important topics that may lead to staff burnout.

The propositions and alternative propositions included in the study guided the initial analysis. Each of the six organizational interventions were explored in the research. The six interventions were explored in the one-on-one interviews and focus group discussions, and as part of the interview topics related to staff burnout. Considerations related to exploring reducing staff-to-client ratios lent to the research proposal.

Reducing Staff-to-Client Ratios

Research findings may include corroboration, extension, or disputation that reducing staff-to-client ratios may decrease staff burnout. I proposed in this study to explore whether the intervention of reducing the staff-to-client ratios will reduce staff burnout. Research findings may not corroborate the proposition that reducing staff-to-client ratios will reduce staff burnout, and reducing staff-to-client ratios may not alleviate staff burnout, or may increase staff burnout. Findings may include alternative perspectives and mixed results whereby reducing staff-to-client ratios reduce burnout for some staff but not for other staff. After administering the BM questionnaire, I conducted one-on-one interviews and a focus group session to explore the perceived affects and implications of the proposed interventions as the interventions relate to staff burnout. Considerations related to making downtime available during the workday lent to the research proposal.

Making Downtime Available during the Workday

Findings may include corroboration and suggest that making downtime available during the workday may decrease staff burnout. Wolfe (1981) defined Downtimes, or time-outs, as the period where staff are able to remove themselves from clients or patients and work on other tasks such as clerical work, and the time periods should be in addition to scheduled breaks or vacations. Several researchers have pointed out that putting in place sanctioned time-outs in stressful day-to-day work is effective in preventing or reducing staff burnout (Collins, 1977; Daley, 1979; Freudenberger, 1977; Maslach, 1976; Mendel, 1979; Pines & Maslach, 1978). As such, making downtime available during the workday was one of the interventions explored in this study on reducing staff burnout. The findings may not corroborate the proposition that making downtime available during the workday will reduce staff burnout, and making downtime available during the workday may not alleviate staff burnout, or may increase staff burnout. The findings may include alternative perspectives and mixed results whereby making downtime available during the workday reduce burnout for some staff but not for other staff. After administering the BM questionnaire, I conducted one-on-one interviews and a focus group session to explore the perceived affects and implications of the proposed interventions as the intervention relates to staff burnout. Considerations related to limiting hours of stressful work lent to the research proposal.

Limiting Hours of Stressful Work

Research findings may include corroboration and suggest that limiting hours of stressful work may decrease staff burnout. Cherniss (1980) found that the stress faced in work is correlated with burnout. The study by Rothmann, Jackson, and Kruge (2003) on local government services found that a higher occupational stress results in higher staff burnout levels. Several, more recent studies, such as that by Mostert and Joubert (2005) that focused on South African police services, and Oginska-Bulik (2006) that focused on health care professions, arrived at the same conclusion that higher work stress leads to elevated burnout levels. However, there also exists evidence that stress does not always lead to burnout (Pines, 2000). As such, this study investigated whether limiting the number of hours of stressful work performed by staff or employees reduces staff burnout levels. The study's findings may not corroborate the proposition that limiting hours of stressful work will reduce staff burnout, and limiting hours of stressful work may not alleviate staff burnout, or may increase staff burnout. The findings may include alternative perspectives and mixed results whereby limiting hours of stressful work may decrease burnout for some staff but not for other staff. After administering the Burnout Measure questionnaire, I conducted one-on-one interviews and a focus group session to explore the perceived affects and implications of the proposed interventions as the intervention relates to staff burnout. Considerations related to increasing organizational flexibility lent to the research proposal.

Increasing Organizational Flexibility

Research findings may include corroboration and suggest that increasing organizational flexibility may decrease staff burnout. Research findings may not corroborate the proposition that increasing organizational flexibility will reduce staff burnout, and increasing organizational flexibility may not decrease staff burnout, or may increase staff burnout. Research findings may include alternative perspectives and mixed results whereby increasing organizational flexibility may decrease burnout for some staff but not for other staff. After administering the BM questionnaire, I conducted one-on-one interviews and a focus group session to explore the perceived affects and implications of the proposed interventions as the intervention related to staff burnout. Considerations related to promoting training opportunities lent to the research proposal.

Promoting Training Opportunities

Research findings may include corroboration and suggest that promoting training opportunities may decrease staff burnout. As posited by Sadovich (2006), employee growth and learning may better prepare employees for more challenging tasks, which may prevent staff burnout levels because employees may be more readily able to face the challenges of client services. Additionally, training employees may enable staff to acquire new skills resulting in improved morale and reduced burnout (Sadovich, 2006). As such, the study will explore whether an intervention of promoting training opportunities will reduce staff burnout. Research findings may not corroborate the proposition that that promoting training opportunities may reduce staff burnout, and promoting training opportunities may not decrease staff burnout, or may increase staff burnout. Research findings may include alternative perspectives and mixed results whereby promoting training opportunities may decrease burnout for some staff but not for other staff. After administering the BM questionnaire, I conducted one-on-one interviews and a focus group session to explore the perceived affects and implications of the proposed interventions as the intervention related to staff burnout. Considerations related to improving work conditions lent to the research proposal.

Improving Work Conditions

Research findings included corroboration and suggest that improving working conditions may decrease staff burnout. According to Sadovich (2006), working conditions include work hours, schedules, monetary rewards, and granting employees the ability to make their own decisions. Poor work conditions were found to lead to dissatisfaction and burnout in employees, especially that of overwork and poor work control (Freeborn, 2001; Maslach, Schaufeli, & Leiter, 2001; Williams & Skinner, 2003). As such, this study explored whether or not improving work conditions reduce staff burnout levels. Research findings may not corroborate the proposition that improving working conditions will reduce staff burnout, and improving working conditions may not decrease staff burnout, or may increase staff burnout. Research findings may include alternative perspectives and mixed results whereby improving working conditions may decrease burnout for some staff but not for other staff. Improving work conditions have already been explored during the interventions of making downtime available during workday, and limiting hours of stressful work. After administering the Burnout Measure questionnaire, I conducted one-on-one interviews and a focus group session to explore the perceived affects and implications of the proposed interventions as the intervention relates to staff burnout. Discussion of the organizational coping strategies follows thusly.

Pines and Aronson's Organizational Coping Strategies

In this study, I specifically addressed the following organizational stress factors presented by Pines and Aronson (1988):

> [The] ratio of the staff to clients, the availability of "time outs" in periods of stress, the amount of time spent in stressful situations, the severity of the problems presented by clients, organizational flexibility, training, positive work conditions, and work significance. (p. 188)

Sample size considerations of this instrument lend to the research proposal.

Sample size

Sample size for qualitative studies is recommended by Creswell (2005) to range from one to 25, and by Polkinghome (2005) to range from five to 25. Alternatively, Yin (2009) noted that the sample size for the mixed methods case design is technically irrelevant. As such, I invited 30 participants to participate in the survey, five participants to participate in the focus group discussion, and two participants to participate in the one-on-one interviews. Instrumentation considerations of the sample size lent to the research proposal.

Instrumentation

The instrumentation that was employed for the purpose of this study included an online, invitation only-staff survey (Appendix A), open-ended semi-structured interviews with staff and administrators (Appendix B) and a focus group with staff (Appendix C). The details of the specific instrumentation tools follow thusly.

The Burnout Measure Questionnaire

The BM is a self-diagnostic tool composed of 21 items with response choices ranging from one to seven, where one represents never and seven represents always (Pines & Aronson, 1988). The BM measurement tool is designed to measure an individual's level of burnout, which can then be correlated with the average level of burnout within the individual's respective organization (Pines & Aronson). Sampling procedure considerations of this instrument lend to the research proposal.

Table 1

Questionnaire Timeframe

	Burnout Measure Questionnaire
Date	January 5, 2014 – January 15, 2014

Sampling Procedures

Using purposive and convenience sampling, clinical, and administrative staff were invited to take the Burnout Measure (BM) questionnaire via an online, confidential, and digitally secure survey administrator (Appendix D). Invitations for the BM questionnaire were sent via email to clinical and administrative staff at the

social service agency in Nevada. Specific demographic

information were collected that exclusively included the

individual's type of position within the company:

Administrative staff or clinical staff. The purpose of the

BM questionnaire was used to determine degrees of staff

burnout. Validity considerations of this instrument lend

to the research proposal.

Validity

The authors of the BM define burnout as "a state

of physical, emotional, and mental exhaustion caused by

long-term involvement in situations that are emotionally

demanding" (Pines and Aronson, p. 8, 1988). While the

definition of burnout by Pines and Aronson (1988) is a

three-dimensional model, the instrument they developed

(BM) consists of a one-dimensional questionnaire,

resulting in a single composite burnout score (Brand,

2007). Additionally, Pines and Aronson (1998) reported

the following regarding construct validity of the BM tool:

"...the burnout measure was examined by correlational analysis with several other theoretically relevant measures; for example, burnout was found to be negatively correlated with self-ratings of satisfaction from work, from life, and from one-self. In one study involving 322 human service professionals, the following correlations between burnout and the three satisfaction measures were found: for satisfaction from work, $r = -.62$, $p < .001$; for satisfaction from life, $r = -.65$, $p < .001$; and for satisfaction from oneself, $r = -.62$, $p < .001$. In all cases the highly significant correlations indicated that the more burned out the professionals were, the less satisfied they were with their work, their lives, and themselves. (p. 221)

The composite burnout scores are presented such that values falling between two and three indicate a good state of well-being, with the cut-off value for an acute crisis being five to seven (Goetzman et al., 2012). Reliability considerations of this instrument lend to the research proposal.

Reliability

Pines and Aronson (1988) identified the following per their extensive research with the BM survey tool:

Test-retest reliability of the measure was found to be .89 for a one-month interval, .76 for a two-month interval, and .66 for a four-month interval. Internal consistency was assessed by the alpha coefficients for most samples studied; the values of the alpha coefficients ranged between .91 and .93. All correlations between the individual items and the composite score were statistically significant at the .001 level of significance in all the studies in which the measure was used. The overall mean value for all samples studies (totaling over 5,000 subjects) was 3.3. A factor analysis gave evidence that the measure assesses a single meaningful construct. (p. 220)

The psychometric qualities of the BM scale were tested to be generally satisfactory. Schaufeli et al. (1998) tested the Cronbach's alpha to be 0.90. Being a generally reliable instrument to test burnout, the BM is used in approximately 5% of all burnout studies (Schaufeli & Enzmann, 1998). Informed consent considerations of this instrument lend to the research proposal.

Informed Consent

Informed consent was required of survey participants prior to participation in the online survey. The study included only adult participants with the physical, mental, and psychological capacity necessary to provide informed consent. Participants were allowed to opt-out at any time without repercussion. Documentation of informed consent was collected and retained for the duration of the data management protocol. Participants acknowledged the purpose of the study, possible benefits and harm, and right to opt out without consequences at any time prior to taking the survey by acknowledging informed consent (Appendix E). Data management protocols follow thusly.

Data Management

Data was held as confidential and not released to any party. Data was stored electronically on a single removable data storage device that was password protected and retained in a secure, locked cabinet and accessible only to the researcher. The data was securely retained for a period of five years in concordance with the APA manual, after which all data will be obliterated. The data collected via the online survey tool was password protected and downloaded to my password-protected computer. Data was analyzed on the same password-protected computer and stored on a password protected data storage device. One-on-one interview considerations

of this instrument lend to the research proposal.

One-on-One Interviews

I gathered information from staff and

administrators through the use of interviews regarding the

six organizational coping strategies identified by Pines

and Aronson (1988). The one-on-one interviews

promoted a conversational style of communicating as

identified and described as important (Gall, Borg, & Gall,

2003). The interviews were important for data collection

due to the unique nature of the interaction between the

participant, interviewer, and the responses to questions,

topics, and to one another (McNamara, 2008). Sampling

procedure considerations of this instrument lend to the

research proposal.

Sampling procedures

An invitation email was sent to staff asking for

participation in the one-on-one interview (Appendix F).

The first two respondents were selected for participation.

Staff who took part in the one-on-one interview did not

participate in the focus group discussion. Validity considerations of this instrument lend to the research proposal.

Validity

The purposive and convenience selection of staff from the available pool is typically regarded as a sound method because, as Yin (2009) noted, the actual sample size is not of relevance for the case study design, and the data that results from the survey sampled "… are assumed to reflect the entire universe or pool, with inferential statistics used to establish confidence intervals for which the representation is presumed accurate" (p. 56). Reliability considerations of this instrument lend to the research proposal.

Reliability

Reliability was bolstered through the use of the case study protocol and the information database (Yin, 2009). The sampling protocol appears replicable. Informed consent considerations of this instrument lend to the research proposal.

Informed Consent

Informed consent was required of interview participants prior to participation in the interview. The study included only adult participants with the physical, mental, and psychological capacity necessary to provide informed consent. Participants were allowed to opt-out at any time without repercussion. Documentation of informed consent was collected prior to the interview and will be retained for the duration of the data management protocol. Participants acknowledged the purpose of the study, possible benefits and harm, and right to opt out without consequences at any time prior to taking the survey by acknowledging informed consent (see appendix E). Validity considerations of this instrument lend to the research proposal.

Validity

Interviews were valid for the case study design because of the in-depth information that may be gleaned during focused, one-on-one interaction (Yin, 2009). The guided conversation of the interview revealed emergent associations between the data from the survey as

compared to the interview (Yin, 2009), or may reveal

alternatively interesting dissimilarities between the data

collection methods, which may contribute to validity.

Validity may be enhanced because the content and topics

discussed may be the same for the three data collection

methods.

Interviews did not pose a challenge for staff due to

my role as a supervisor within the agency. Staff were not

reluctant to share information with me during the

interview regarding burnout, and staff did not downplay

the prevalence of burnout. Staff did not provide limited

information on the topic of staff burnout during the

interview. Reliability considerations of this instrument

lend to the research proposal.

Reliability

The reliability of the interview may be beneficial

due to the "… consistent line of inquiry" (Yin, 2009, p.

106), and because the consistent protocols used for the

study appear replicable. A weakness of the interview may

include the lack of standardized interview questions.

Data management considerations of this instrument lend

to the research proposal.

Data Management

Data was held as confidential and not released to

any party. Data was stored electronically on a single

removable data storage device that was password

protected and retained in a secure, locked cabinet and

accessible only to the researcher. Research data was

securely retained for a period of five years in accordance

with current guidelines for conducting research with

human participants guidelines, after which all data will be

obliterated.

Interview data was collected via an MP3 voice

recording device that was pre-disclosed, in plain sight,

and clearly visible to the interviewee. Voice recordings

were processed by a secure and confidential third party

transcription service. Voice recordings and transcriptions

were managed in accordance with the above listed

security protocol. Interviewees were asked to review

their interview transcripts for possible corrections. Focus

group discussion considerations of this study lend to the

research proposal.

Focus Group Discussion

I gathered data from staff through the use of a

focus group regarding the six organizational coping

strategies identified by Pines and Aronson (1988). The

focus group discussion elicited data that was different

from what one individual can provide because the

members of the group may initiate discussion topics and

spur further conversation that had not been previously

explored by any one individual (Bratton, Grint & Nelson,

2005; Shockley-Zalabak, 2009; Zastrow, 2009). The

group conversational style of communication has been

identified as important for research purposes (Gall, Borg,

& Gall, 2003). Sampling procedure considerations of this

instrument lend to the research proposal.

Sampling Procedures

An invitation email was sent to staff asking for

participation in the focus group discussion (Appendix G).

The first two respondents were selected for participation.

Staff who took part in the focus group discussion did not

take part in the one-on-one interview. Validity

considerations of this instrument lend to the research

proposal.

Validity

The focus group conversational style of

communication may be important as posited by Gall,

Gall, and Borg (2003), and the back-and-forth nature of

the group discussion may enhance the data that was

gathered via the other two data collection methods.

Validity may be enhanced because the content and topics

discussed may be the same for all three data collection

methods (Gall, Borg, & Gall).

Focus group discussions did not pose a challenge

for staff due to my role as a supervisor within the agency.

Staff were not reluctant to share information with me

during the focus group discussions regarding burnout, and

did not downplay the prevalence of burnout. Staff did not

provide only limited information on the topic of staff

burnout during the interview. Staff did not disagree with each other regarding staff burnout. Reliability considerations of this instrument lend to the research proposal.

Reliability

The reliability of the focus group discussion may be beneficial due to the "… consistent line of inquiry" (Yin, 2009, p. 106), and because the consistent protocols used for the study appear replicable. A weakness of the focus group may include the lack of specific discussion questions, but the semi-structured question and answer format has been deemed appropriate for focus groups and appears replicable (Leedy & Ormrod, 2005). Informed consent considerations of this instrument lend to the research proposal.

Informed Consent

Informed consent was required of focus group discussion participants prior to participation in the interview. The study included only adult participants with the physical, mental, and psychological capacity necessary to provide informed consent. Participants were allowed to opt-out at any time without repercussion. Documentation of informed consent was collected prior to the focus group discussion and was retained for the duration of the data management protocol. Participants acknowledged the purpose of the study, possible benefits and harm, and the right to opt out without consequences at any time prior to taking the survey by acknowledging informed consent (Appendix E). Data management considerations of this instrument lend to the research proposal.

Data Management

Data was held as confidential and not released to any party. Data was stored electronically on a single removable data storage device that was password protected and retained in a secure, locked cabinet and accessible only to me. Research data will be securely retained for a period of five years in accordance with the APA manual, after which all data will be obliterated.

Focus group discussion data was collected via an MP3 voice recording device that was pre-disclosed, in plain sight, and visible to the participants. Voice recordings were transcribed by a professional and confidential third party transcription service. Voice recordings and transcriptions were managed in accordance with the above listed security protocol. Participants were asked to review their interview transcripts for possible corrections. Data analysis considerations follow thusly.

Data Analysis

Data analysis consisted of (a) quantitative data analysis procedure; (b) qualitative data analysis procedure; (c) contrast; (d) interview coding and re-coding; (e) abstraction; (f) triangulation; and (g) the study sequence of events. Quantitative data analysis procedures and considerations lend to the research proposal.

Quantitative Data Analysis Procedure

I conducted descriptive data analysis using Survey Monkey by processing and downloading means and standard deviation by (a) groups (administrative and support staff, (b) metric themes, and (c) aggregate scoring. Qualitative data analysis procedures and considerations lend to the research proposal.

Qualitative Data Analysis Procedure

I used NVivo software to code and sort the qualitative data that is accumulated during the one-on-one interviews and focus group. NVivo software provided a standardized method for analyzing the qualitative data, and assisted in identifying themes and emergent themes. The qualitative portion of the study included methods necessary to identify propositions and alternate propositions. Through iterative reviews, themes developed via contrasting grouped themes with stakeholder roles, research methods, and other emergent characterizations. Contrast procedures and considerations lend to the research proposal.

Contrast

I contrasted the findings of this mixed methods case study against the stated and emerging propositions for corroborating, disputing, or extending the findings of Pines and Aronson's (1988) study with regards to the possible staff burnout interventions that can be applied at the organizational level, to include: (a) reducing staff-to-client ratios, (b) making downtime available during the workday, (c) limiting hours of stressful work, (d) increasing organizational flexibility, (e) promoting training opportunities, and (f) improving work conditions. Using NVivo software applications, the qualitative data analysis were coded, categorized, and abstracted. One-on-one interviews and focus group discussions were analyzed qualitatively in the same manner, but they were performed separate from one another, each having their own analysis prior to triangulation. Coding and re-coding procedures and considerations lend to the research proposal.

Coding and Re-coding of Interviews

One-on-one interviews and focus group discussions were coded. Open coding was used where general themes or categories within each one-on-one interview and focus group discussion were identified.

The open coding process is, according to Strauss and Corbin (1990), the ability to break down, examine, compare, conceptualize, and categorize data. Coding may be used to help organize data and identify patterns based upon the structure of the associated patterns (Auerbach & Silverstein, 2003). The codes may become the labels to assign meaning to the qualitative information collected during the course of the study. Using the codes, I collated the relevant information from the transcribed interviews and focus group discussions (Miles & Huberman, 1994). I included a single case study approach, and the themes within the case study were evaluated (Lincoln & Guba, 1985). Coding the research allows the reader to identify themes and first-hand accounts of participants that explain their experiences regarding themes and emergent themes. The coding and re-coding procedures will follow Krippendorff's (2004) analytic questions and include:

1. Which data are analyzed?

2. How are they defined?

3. What is the population from which they are

   drawn?

4. What is the context relative to which the data are

   analyzed?

5. What are the boundaries of the analysis?

6. What is the target of the inferences?

Abstraction procedures and considerations lend to the

research proposal.

Abstraction

The abstraction of data from the study allowed me

to understand the topic (Morse & Richards, 2002), while

allowing the reader a broader picture of the results of the

data. I analyzed the concepts to extract the general

concepts out of the specific concepts. This step of the

qualitative analysis helped isolate an aspect, aspects, or

differing aspects of a concept so as to provide the

concepts with clarity and precision. The purpose of the

abstraction in this study was be to give the reader an

overview of each theme and emergent theme to help the

reader understand the information gleaned from the data.

Triangulation procedures and considerations lend to the research proposal.

Triangulation

To aid in bolstering the validity of the study, data triangulation was used to facilitate the multiple data gathering methods, and was used to combine the data from multiple sources and methods of analysis. Source method triangulation may bolster the validity of the data by offsetting the data sources and triangulation. According the Hastings (2010), triangulation refers to the practice of analyzing multiple data sources, which may enhance the credibility of a research study. Further, Yin (2009) refers to the use of triangulation as a means for investigating the "converging lines of inquiry" (p. 115) that are intrinsic to the case study process.

After performing quantitative and qualitative analysis separately, the qualitative and quantitative data were brought together by converging (contrasting) the results that were acquired during the interpretation phase and involves the process of triangulation. Qualitative data included analysis of the interviews and the focus group discussion, and quantitative data analysis explored means and standard deviation by (a) groups (administrative and support staff, (b) metric themes, and (c) aggregate scoring. The two sets of results were merged during the data interpretation phase of the study. The purpose of data triangulation and interpretation includes drawing conclusions about a research problem. I sought to identify themes in the qualitative data during the analysis and extrapolate on the results by exploring the participants' responses in-depth (Rossman & Wilson, 1985; Tashakkori & Teddie, 1998; Creswell, 2003). This should increase the validity of the conclusions drawn and possibly provide potential direction for future research. Sequence of study events procedures and considerations lend to the research proposal.

Sequence of Study Events

I notified the participants of the purpose and scope of the study at the onset of the research (Appendix E). All participants were notified of the voluntary nature of the study (Appendix E). Table 2 summarizes the

sequence of the study's events.

Table 2

Sequence of Formal Research Events

	December	**January**
Notification	January 15, 2013	
Questionnaire		February 15, 2014
Interviews		February 20, 2014
Focus Group		February 21, 2014

Ethical Considerations

Denscombe (2007) related that full disclosure of

the purpose of the survey, interview, and focus group

session may be necessary for participants in a focus group

and qualitative study. Informed consent included

disclosures of the use of recording devices during the

interviews and focus group discussion for the purpose of

documentation and transcription. The informed consent

form noted that there was to be no foreseeable risk for

participation in the study. All pertinent contact

information for the researcher and the university were

included in the informed consent form in the event that

any questions arise from the participants in the study. I

did not collect or disclose the names or identities of the respondents during any part of the study in order to protect the privacy of participants. Interview identification numbers were used to distinguish the interview and focus group responses.

For the purposes of the study, I limited any study related interactions with staff to the confines of the specified study period. There were not any discussion of the study online survey, focus group, or interviews other than during the time established to conduct these sessions for data collection. Once the data collection process ceased, the participants ceased to be such. Ethical considerations for each of the research methods will follow thusly.

Online Survey

Informed consent was required of survey participants prior to participation in the online survey. The study included only adult participants with the physical, mental, and psychological capacity necessary to provide informed consent. Participants were allowed to opt-out at any time without repercussion. Documentation of informed consent was collected and will be retained for the duration of the data management protocol. Participants acknowledged the purpose of the study, possible benefits and harm, and right to opt out without consequences at any time prior to taking the survey by acknowledging informed consent (Appendix E). Ethical considerations for one-on-one interviews lend to the research proposal.

One-on-One Interviews

Informed consent was required of interview participants prior to participation in the interview. The study included only adult participants with the physical, mental, and psychological capacity necessary to provide informed consent. Participants were allowed to opt-out at any time without repercussion. Documentation of informed consent was collected prior to the interview and will be retained for the duration of the data management protocol. Participants acknowledged the purpose of the study, possible benefits and harm, and right to opt out without consequences at any time prior to taking the survey by acknowledging informed consent (Appendix E). Ethical considerations for focus group discussions lend to the research proposal.

Focus Group Discussion

Informed consent was required of focus group discussion participants prior to participation in the interview. The study included only adult participants with the physical, mental, and psychological capacity necessary to provide informed consent. Participants were allowed to opt-out at any time without repercussion. Documentation of informed consent was collected prior to the focus group discussion and will be retained for the duration of the data management protocol. Participants acknowledged the purpose of the study, possible benefits and harm, and right to opt out without consequences at any time prior to taking the survey by acknowledging informed consent (Appendix E). Validity procedures and considerations lend to the research proposal.

Validity

The four primary tenets of validity were identified by Lincoln and Guba (1985) and include truth value, applicability, consistency, and neutrality, whereby the theoretical framework for this proposal includes positivist and interpretive inquiry method, and reframes the points for use in interpretive methodologies. Truth value appears to be integral to understanding validity. Truth value procedures and considerations lend to the research proposal.

Truth Value

Truth value refers to methods for establishing confidence in the truth of a researcher's study findings regarding the subjects, and confidence in the findings of the study may be explored when the context of where the study took place is known (Lincon & Guba, 1985). The concept of truth value as stated by Lincoln and Guba (1985) has also been explained as relating to internal validity and was further developed and explained by Cook and Campbell (1979). The positivist methodologists

Pedhazur and Schmelkin (1991) identified that the eight

criteria of truth value may include: (a) history, (b)

maturation, (c) testing, (d) instrumentation, (e) regression

to the mean, (f) selection, (g) mortality, (h) diffusion or

imitation of treatments, and (i) compensatory rivalry or

resentful demoralization. Several methods to increase

probability of credible findings were outlined by Lincoln

and Guba. These methods, according to Lincoln and

Guba may include (a) lengthy interaction and consistent

observation of participants, (b) triangulation of data

sources, (c) efforts to build rapport and trust with

participants, (d) peer debriefing after data gathering, (e)

participant case analysis, (f) referential adequacy and

documentation of data, (g) member checks, and (h)

presenting findings to participants for confirmation and

revision of understanding. Applicability considerations

lend to the research proposal.

Applicability

Applicability was described by Lincoln and Guba

(1985) as the extent to which findings from one study

may be applicable to other studies or contexts. This concept may have been extrapolated from the positivist conceptualization of external validity. External validity refers to the ability to generalize findings across different populations, locations, settings, and times (Lincoln & Guba, 1985). Smaller studies with varied samples may relate more to applicability as noted by Cook and Campbell (as cited in Pedhazur & Schmelkin, 1991). Interpretive researchers do not relate that applicability is reasonably generalized beyond situations with similar contexts, whereas positivist researchers may seek to generalize across differing populations, situations, or contexts (Pedhazur & Schmelkin, 1991). Lincoln and Guba described that interpretive researchers are most typically interested in the transferability of findings to other contexts, but in order to achieve such transferability a rich description of the context of the study may be required. Shenton (2004) posited that the mixed method case study and its environment may be better understood by the researcher, and that the participants may have an emergent understanding of the case study topic for such understanding to be transferred to real life contexts. Consistency procedures and considerations lend to the research proposal.

Consistency

Exploring consistency may help determine the extent to which findings from a study might be repeated if the study was to be replicated with like subjects or in a similar context (Lincoln & Guba, 1985). The concept of consistency may be related to reliability in the positivist tradition. While reliability may be discussed separately from validity, reliability may be an insufficient but necessary condition of developing reliable inferences from a positivist or post-positivist study (Lincoln & Guba). Methods to help ensure consistency may take place through an audit trail (Houser, 2012). To perform this task, every aspect of the proposed study should be analyzed by the researcher and consideration given to every part of the process (Yin, 2009). By performing a thorough inventory of the steps taken in the proposed research process, consistency should be high (Yin). Thoroughly examining the steps in the proposed research should allow future researchers to follow the steps detailed in the proposed research, and duplicate them in future studies (Yin). Additionally, consistency should be assessed through triangulation, which may be of particular importance for the mixed methods case study design (Yin). Neutrality procedures and considerations lend to the research proposal.

Neutrality

Neutrality is the method by which the findings of a study may be influenced solely by the participants and subject matter of the study, and not by the motives or biases of the researcher (Lincoln & Guba, 1985). While the concept of neutrality may overlap with the positivist ideal of objectivity, it may also differ in several important ways. In the positivist tradition, objectivity relates that reality or truth may exist to be discovered and is typically sought through distance between the observer and the observed (Lincoln & Guba). The participants were voluntarily selected for this research study which should

lend credibility to the proposed research project. Full

disclosure of the goals and aims of the study were given

to the participants prior to their consent or signing and

answering of the research questions (Appendix E).

Debriefing sessions between the researcher and

participants was conducted during the data gathering

phase of the research study to help ensure the integrity of

the questions asked and to help assess whether or not the

research study participants believe the research study

questions to be non-biased and non-judgmental. Propriety

of methodology considerations lend to the research

proposal.

Propriety of Methodology

Methodology and research design are generally

the two primary components of a study because they may

guide the researcher in carrying out the goal of the study

with accurate results (Yin, 2009). The design of the

methodology may be considered to be the foundation of

the collection, measurement, and analyses of data (Burns

& Groves, 2001; Cooper & Schindler, 2008). I utilized a mixed-methods case study approach where I sought to identify propositions and alternative propositions. The mixed methods approach was used because the purpose of the evaluation was to determine the general appropriateness of the methodology. The chapter summary follows thusly.

Summary

This chapter included explanation of the research methodology and design, the research questions and propositions, the unit of analysis, sample size, instrumentation and data collection, and the data analysis methodology that was used for this study. This mixed methods, explanatory case study, appears to be appropriate to determine if the Pines and Aronson (1988) burnout prevention and intervention strategies are effective at reducing burnout for social services staff.

CHAPTER FOUR: FINDINGS

Using a mixed methods, explanatory, single-case study design, I explored the efficacy of the organizational burnout prevention methods posited by Pines and Aronson (1988). Staff interviews, focus group, and online surveys were used for data gathering and to identify themes and emergent themes from propositional analysis. After explaining the purpose of the study, research questions, propositions, and data collection procedures, analysis of the findings is provided.

Restatement of the Purpose

The purpose of this mixed methods case study was to explore specific organizational coping strategies for preventing burnout from the Pines and Aronson (1988) model of burnout intervention and prevention strategies at Youth Services (YS), located in the southwestern United States. YS provide community-based behavioral health and social services to youth and families and employs more than 200 social service professionals. I used the mixed methods case study approach to study burnout within the organization (Yin, 2009). The research phase of the study incorporated quantitative and qualitative methods through anonymous, invitation-only online surveys to collect the data from the Burnout Measure (Pines & Aronson, 2008) and from open-ended questions asked during in-person interviews and a focus group. The study yielded corroboration of some aspects of the burnout prevention and intervention strategies as posited by Pines and Aronson (1988), and expanded upon additional strategies not previously mentioned. The following research questions guided the study.

Research Questions

The following questions guided the research:

RQ1: How prevalent is staff burnout within the agency?

RQ2: How well do the six organizational interventions of (a) reducing staff-to-client ratios, (b) making downtime available during the workday, (c) limiting hours of stressful work, (d) increasing organizational flexibility, (e) promoting training opportunities, (f) and improving work conditions presented by Pines and Aronson (1988) characterize prevention and alleviation of staff burnout within the social services agency?

Logic Linking Data to the Propositions

Yin (2009) posited that a desirable technique for case study analysis is pattern-matching logic linking data to related propositions. Based upon the results of the BM assessment to explore the level of staff burnout, and the efficacy of Pines and Aronson's organizational burnout prevention strategies, the results of the data collected were evaluated for the purposes of measuring staff burnout and the propositions, alternative propositions, themes, and emergent themes as related to burnout prevention and intervention strategies (Pines & Aronson,

1988). Subsequent findings were factored when assessing

propositions, alternate propositions, themes, and emergent

themes. Pines and Aronson's six organizational burnout

interventions include (a) reducing staff-to-client ratios, (b)

making downtime available during the workday, (c)

limiting hours of stressful work, (d) increasing

organizational flexibility, (e) promoting training

opportunities, (f) and improving work conditions. This

study included the inputs from Pines and Aronson's

(1988) study as basis of the propositions. Propositions

included:

1. Reducing staff-to-client ratios should decrease staff burnout.

2. Making downtime available during the workday should decrease staff burnout.

3. Limiting hours of stressful work should decrease staff burnout.

4. Increasing organizational flexibility should decrease staff burnout.

5. Promoting training opportunities should decrease staff burnout.

6. Improving work conditions should decrease staff burnout.

Alternate propositions may identify themes not previously identified by Pines and Aronson (1988) and may include:

1. Proposed interventions may temporarily decrease staff burnout, may not decrease staff burnout, or may increase staff burnout.

2. Emergent themes to include alternate interventions to decrease staff burnout may develop. Examples of emergent themes to decrease staff burnout may include the efficacy of group work or project sharing, leveraging staff from different departments to assist with non-routine tasks, or weekly strategy sessions to discuss important topics that may lead to staff burnout.

The propositions and alternative propositions included in the study guided the initial analysis. Each of the six organizational interventions were explored in the research. The six interventions were explored through one-on-one interviews and a focus group discussion. In this study I specifically addressed the following organizational stress factors presented by Pines and Aronson (1988):

[The] ratio of the staff to clients, the availability of "time outs" in periods of stress, the amount of time spent in stressful situations, the severity of the problems presented by clients, organizational flexibility, training, positive work conditions, and work significance. (p. 188)

Review of Data Collection Procedures

Sample Size

I invited 30 participants to participate in the online survey, five participants to participate in the focus group discussion, and three to participate in the one-on-one interviews. Instrumentation considerations of the sample size lent to the research.

Instrumentation

The instrumentation that I used for this study included an online, invitation only, staff survey (Appendix A), open-ended semi-structured interviews with staff and administrators (Appendix B) and a focus group session with staff (Appendix C). The details of the specific instrumentation tools follow thusly.

Burnout Measure Online Survey

The BM is a self-diagnostic tool composed of 21 items with response choices ranging from one to seven, where one represents never and seven represents always (Pines & Aronson, 1988). The BM measurement tool was designed to measure an individual's level of burnout, which can then be correlated with the average level of burnout within the individual's respective organization (Pines & Aronson).

Using purposive and convenience sampling, clinical, and administrative staff were invited to take the Burnout Measure (BM) questionnaire via an online, confidential, and digitally secure survey administrator (Appendix D). Invitations for the BM questionnaire were sent via email to clinical and administrative staff at the social service agency in Nevada. Specific demographic information was collected to exclusively include the individual's type of position within the company: Administrative staff or clinical staff. The purpose of the

BM questionnaire was used to determine degree of staff burnout.

One-on-One Staff Interviews

I gathered information from staff and administrators using interviews regarding the six organizational coping strategies identified by Pines and Aronson (1988). The one-on-one interviews promoted a conversational style of communicating as identified and described as important (Gall et al., 2003). The interviews were important for data collection due to the unique nature of the interaction between the participant, interviewer, and the responses to questions, topics, and to one another (McNamara, 2008).

An invitation email was sent to staff asking for participation in the one-on-one interview (Appendix F). The first two respondents were selected for participation. Staff who took part in the one-on-one interview did not participate in the focus group discussion. The following questions were asked during the one-on-one interviews:

1. Bearing in mind the six organizational coping strategies for reducing and preventing staff burnout as described by Pines and Aronson (1988) to include (a) reducing staff-to-client ratios, (b) making downtime available during the workday, (c) limiting hours of stressful work, (d) increasing organizational flexibility, (e) promoting training opportunities, (f) and improving work conditions, which strategy or strategies do you believe would be the most beneficial for staff at this agency?

2. Why do you believe that specific strategy or strategies will be effective for reducing and preventing staff burnout?
   a. How did you come to that point of view?

3. What burnout prevention and intervention strategy or strategies do you believe would be beneficial for staff at this agency that are not included in this list?
   a. How did you come to that point of view?

4. What factor or factors do you believe contribute to staff burnout at this agency that we have not already discussed?
   a. Why do you believe that to be true?

Focus Group Discussion

I gathered data from staff using a focus group session regarding the six organizational coping strategies identified by Pines and Aronson (1988). The focus group discussion elicited data and information that was somewhat different from the individual interviews. The group conversational style of communication was

important for research purposes.

An invitation email was sent to staff asking for

participation in the focus group discussion (Appendix G).

The first four respondents were selected for participation.

Staff who took part in the focus group discussion did not

take part in the one-on-one interview. The following

questions were asked during the focus group discussion:

1. Bearing in mind the six organizational coping strategies for reducing and preventing staff burnout as described by Pines and Aronson (1988) to include (a) reducing staff-to-client ratios, (b) making downtime available during the workday, (c) limiting hours of stressful work, (d) increasing organizational flexibility, (e) promoting training opportunities, (f) and improving work conditions, which strategy or strategies do you believe would be the most beneficial for staff at this agency?

2. Why do you believe that specific strategy will be effective for reducing and preventing staff burnout?

3. What burnout prevention and intervention strategy or strategies do you believe would be beneficial for staff at this agency that are not included in this list?

4. What factors of factors do you believe contribute to staff burnout at this agency that we have not already discussed?

Findings

Detailed explanations of each data set follow. Themes, emergent themes, propositions, and alternative positions are described thereafter. Specific case study data is located in Appendices .

Pines and Aronson's (1988) six organizational burnout prevention and intervention strategies include (a) reducing staff-to-client ratios, (b) making downtime available during the workday, (c) limiting hours of stressful work, (d) increasing organizational flexibility, (e) promoting training opportunities, (f) and improving work conditions. The following table shows the actual prevention and intervention strategies as identified by staff during the interviews and focus group.

Table 3

Most Commonly Identified Staff Burnout Prevention and

Intervention Strategies

Intervention and Prevention Strategy	Prevalence of Identification by Staff
Reducing staff-to-client ratios	First most commonly identified
Making downtime available during the workday	Not identified
Limiting hours of stressful work	Not identified
Increasing organizational flexibility	Not identified
Promoting training opportunities	Second most commonly identified
Improving work conditions	Third most commonly identified

Staff Burnout Online Survey

The Burnout Measure was administered online to

twenty participants on an invitation only basis. The

online survey consisted of twenty-one questions that were

designed to measure the respondents' personal level of

job burnout. The survey utilized a Likert scale of 1 to 7

with the following rating scale: 1 – never, 2 – once in a

great while, 3 – rarely, 4 – sometimes, 5 – often, 6 –

usually, 7 – always. The Burnout Measure assessment

data associated with each survey question are listed

below.

Table 4

Descriptive Assessment of Overall Stress

N=20	M	SD
1. How often do you experience: Being Tired?	5.30	0.97
2: How often do you experience: Feeling Depressed?	3.85	1.26
3: How often do you experience: Having a Good Day?	4.50	0.94
4: How often do you experience: Being Physically Exhausted	4.40	1.09
5: How often do you experience: Being Emotionally Exhausted?	4.65	0.98
6: How often do you experience: Being Happy?	4.50	0.88
7: How often do you experience: Being "Wiped Out?"	4.30	0.97
8: How often do you experience: "Can't take it anymore?"	3.65	1.22
9: How often do you experience: Being Unhappy?	4.05	1.09
10: How often do you experience: Feeling Run-Down?	3.95	1.09
11: How often do you experience: Feeling Trapped?	3.90	1.48
12: How often do you experience: Feeling Worthless?	2.65	1.49
13: How often do you experience: Being Weary?	3.30	1.55
14: How often do you experience: Being Troubled?	3.10	1.41
15. How often do you experience: Feeling Disillusioned and Resentful?	3.40	1.78
16: How often do you experience: Being Weak and Susceptible to Illness?	3.15	1.38
17: How often do you experience: Feeling	2.70	1.52

Hopeless?		
18: How often do you experience: Feeling Rejected?	2.70	1.17
19: How often do you experience: Feeling Optimistic?	4.20	1.15
20: How often do you experience: Feeling Energetic?	3.70	0.97
21: How often do you experience: Feeling Anxious?	4.10	1.25

The Burnout Measure scores that are listed in the table above are tabulated based upon the mathematical formula that can be found on the Burnout Measure self assessment in appendix A. While the individual scores of each question may be informative, the individual scores do not measure or gauge the level of overall staff burnout. The overall measurement of staff burnout is based upon the following rating scale per the tabulation of the entire Burnout Measure instrument as described by Pines and Aronson (1988). This overall score falls within what may be considered the normal range, yet some action may be necessary for certain individual staff who may have scored higher than the overall average indicates. Emergent themes follow accordingly.

Emergent Themes

The focus group and one-on-one interviews yielded corroboration of three of the organizational coping strategies to reduce and prevent staff burnout as posited by Pines and Aronson (1988), and are listed here in order of prevalence from most to least in prominence: (a) reducing staff-to-client ratios, (b) promoting training opportunities, and (c) improving work conditions. The proposed interventions that were not addressed, or noted, as being important for reducing or preventing staff burnout include: (a) making downtime available the workday, (b) limiting hours of stressful work, and (c) increasing organizational flexibility. The three corroborated strategies are discussed as follows.

Reducing Staff-To-Client Ratios

High and continually increasing staff-to-client ratios was the most prevalent contributor to staff burnout as reported during the focus group and interviews. Staff reported that the high ratios contribute generally to burnout because this factor affects all staff at all levels, but more specifically, it has deleterious implications for

all job duties. Specific areas that were reported by staff to

be affected by the high staff-to-client ratios include (a)

not being able to provide clients with the required

services, (b) inability to participate in training

opportunities due to a high workload, (c) lack of time to

engage in self-care; specifically, taking breaks during the

workday as well as a dedicated lunch period, (d) lack of

training on proper self-care techniques, and (e) poor

overall work quality.

Promoting Training Opportunities

Staff reported during the focus group and one-on-

one interviews that training opportunities are generally

lacking in terms of frequency of offering and availability.

Staff also reported that training is not promoted by the

agency as being important as evidenced by the lack of

training opportunities within the agency as well as an

overall lack of encouragement to attend available training

opportunities in the community. Additionally, staff

reported that because of the high staff-to-client ratios, and because staff pay is directly associated with the staff-to-client ratios, the ability of staff to take unpaid time to attend training opportunities is financially stressful for staff and not promoted by the agency due to lost billable services and reduced revenue and productivity for the agency.

Improving Work Conditions

While the two aforementioned organizational coping strategies may be regarded within the industry as self-explanatory, the strategies are also defined by Pines and Aronson (1988). Conversely, the strategy of improving work conditions is loosely defined and more nebulous than the others. Pines and Aronson noted that improving work conditions may be as simple as offering comfortable chairs or pleasing wall colors, or as complex as reducing bureaucratic interference, implementing a rewards system, or helping staff gain a sense of significance from their work.

Overall themes reported by staff during the focus group session and one-on-one interviews include (a) a lack of understanding and engagement of day-to-day operations of offices by upper level management, (b) expectations of staff and managers by upper level management that are incongruent with the actual operations of the offices and office staff, (c) reported lack of interest in learning about the daily operations of offices by upper level management, (d) lack of general as well as specific guidance and support from upper level management, (e) the mission statement is not supported by the organization, (f) lack of appreciation, acknowledgement and recognition for hard work; (g) a generally poor pay scale and no pay raises for staff, (h) broken promises on the part of upper level management, (i) lack of proper staffing levels, (j) poor work environment due to lack of team cohesion or sense of belonging within the organization, and (k) perceived focus on billable services, revenue, and the bottom line profits above all else on the part of upper level management and the organization as a whole.

Alternate Propositions

During the focus group and interviews, staff reported that staff pay is tied directly to the billable services they provide. One hour of billable services equates to one hour of pay. If staff is not providing billable services, or if billable services are reduced, then staff pay is reduced accordingly. Staff reported that this pay model is a significant stressor and a leading factor in staff burnout. Staff reported feeling great pressure to bill all possible services so as to not have their pay affected, even if that meant that staff sacrificed in other areas to include not taking time for self-care and occasionally focusing quantity of services rendered instead of quality. Staff also reported that because pay is directly associated with billable services, that any training they might participate in would be on their own time and not paid. Staff reported that due to the low hourly wage, what some referred to as not being a living wage, they would not be able to skip any billable time to participate in training during work hours which is when many community training sessions are offered.

Summary

A mixed methods, explanatory, single-case study design to explore the efficacy of the organizational burnout prevention and intervention methods as posited by Pines and Aronson (1988) was employed. Staff interviews, focus group, and online surveys were used for data gathering and to identify themes and emergent themes from propositional analysis. Corroboration of the model presented by Pines and Aronson was evident, and emergent themes developed. Considering the corroboration of the model and emergent themes, I will review the findings, propose solutions to identified problems, and suggest implications and recommendations for future studies.

CHAPTER FIVE: SUMMARY, CONCLUSIONS,

AND RECOMMENDATIONS

Using a mixed methods, explanatory, single-case study design, I explored the efficacy of the organizational burnout prevention methods posited by Pines and Aronson (1988). Staff interviews, focus group, and online surveys were used for data gathering and to identify themes and emergent themes, and propositions and alternative propositions guided the initial analysis. After explaining the purpose of the study and associated discussion, ethical concerns, propositions and alternate propositions, and conclusions, I will address implications, recommendations, and suggested future research.

Purpose of the Study

The purpose of this mixed methods case study was to explore specific organizational coping strategies for preventing burnout from the Pines and Aronson (1988) model of burnout intervention and prevention strategies at Youth Services (YS), located in the southwestern United States. YS provide community-based behavioral health and social services to youth and families and employs more than 200 social service professionals. I used the mixed methods case study approach to study burnout within the organization (Yin, 2009). The research phase of the study incorporated quantitative and qualitative methods through anonymous, invitation-only online surveys to collect the data from the Burnout Measure (Pines & Aronson, 2008) and from open-ended questions asked during in-person interviews and a focus group. The study yielded corroboration of some aspects of the burnout prevention and intervention strategies as posited by Pines and Aronson (1988), and expanded upon additional strategies not previously mentioned. Discussion of the research follows.

Discussion

Using the mixed-methods case study design, I explored the organizational strategies for preventing and alleviating staff burnout as posited by Pines and Aronson (1988). I administered the Burnout Measure as an online survey to staff to determine the overall level of staff burnout, and then conducted individual interviews and a focus group with staff to elicit feedback regarding the organizational strategies that Pines and Aronson deemed effective for preventing and alleviating staff burnout. Propositions and alternate propositions were evident in the research, and emergent themes arose from staff observations and feedback. The research findings corroborated and extended the strategies posited by Pines and Aronson.

The Burnout Measure survey indicated the overall level of staff burnout to be 2.28, which is deemed to be in the acceptable range and a relatively low risk for burnout. However, it should be noted that this is an average score and individual levels of burnout may differ, some being scores being higher and some lower. The focus group and interviews yielded corroboration that reducing staff-to-client ratios, promoting training opportunities, and improving work conditions may be important factors for reducing and preventing staff burnout. Alternatively, making downtime available during the workday, limiting hours of stressful work, and increasing organizational

flexibility were not corroborated as being important

factors for reducing or preventing staff burnout.

Emergent themes discovered during the research include

the following: (a) a lack of understanding and engagement

of day-to-day operations of offices by upper level

management; (b) expectations of staff and managers by

upper level management that are incongruent with the

actual operations of the offices and office staff; (c)

reported lack of interest in learning about the daily

operations of offices by upper level management; (d) lack

of general as well as specific guidance and support from

upper level management; (e) the mission statement is not

supported by the organization; (f) lack of appreciation,

acknowledgement and recognition for hard work; (g) a

generally poor pay scale and no pay raises for staff; (h)

broken promises on the part of upper level management;

(i) lack of proper staffing levels; (j) poor work

environment due to lack of team cohesion or sense of

belonging within the organization; and (k) perceived

focus on billable services, revenue, and the bottom line profits above all else on the part of upper level management and the organization as a whole.

During the focus group and interviews, staff reported that staff pay is related directly to the billable services they provide. One hour of billable services equates to one hour of pay. If staff is not providing billable services, or if billable services are reduced, then staff pay is reduced accordingly. Staff reported that this pay model is a significant stressor and a leading factor in staff burnout. Staff reported feeling great pressure to bill all possible services so as to not have their pay affected, even if that meant that staff sacrificed in other areas to include not taking time for self-care and occasionally focusing quantity of services rendered instead of quality. Staff also reported that because pay is directly associated with billable services, that any training they might participate in would be on their own time and not paid. Staff reported that due to the low hourly wage, what some referred to as not being a living wage, they would not be able to skip any billable time to participate in training during work hours, which is when many community training sessions are offered.

Ethical Considerations

Denscombe (2007) related that full disclosure of the purpose of the survey, interview, and focus group session may be necessary for participants in a focus group and qualitative study. Informed consent included disclosures of the use of recording devices during the interviews and focus group discussion for the purpose of documentation and transcription. The informed consent form noted that there was no foreseeable risk for participation in the study. All pertinent contact information for the researcher and the university were included in the informed consent form in the event that any questions arose from the participants in the study. I did not collect, or disclose, the names or identities of the respondents during any part of the study in order to protect the privacy of participants. Identification numbers were used to distinguish the interview and focus group responses.

For the purpose of the study, I limited study related interactions with staff to the confines of the specified study period. There was not any discussion of the study online survey, focus group, or interviews other than during the time established to conduct these sessions for data collection. Once the data collection process ceased, the participants ceased to be such.

Propositions and Alternate Propositions

This study included the inputs from Pines and Aronson's (1988) study as basis of the propositions. Propositions included:

1. Reducing staff-to-client ratios should decrease staff burnout.

2. Making downtime available during the workday should decrease staff burnout.

3. Limiting hours of stressful work should decrease staff burnout.

4. Increasing organizational flexibility should decrease staff burnout.

5. Promoting training opportunities should decrease staff burnout.

6. Improving work conditions should decrease staff burnout.

Alternate propositions may identify themes not previously identified by Pines and Aronson (1988) and may include:

1. Proposed interventions may temporarily decrease staff burnout, may not decrease staff burnout, or may increase staff burnout.

2. Emergent themes to include alternate interventions to decrease staff burnout may develop. Examples of emergent themes to decrease staff burnout may include the efficacy of group work or project sharing, leveraging staff from different departments to assist with non-routine tasks, or weekly strategy sessions to discuss important topics that may lead to staff burnout.

Conclusions

The case study conclusions are related in order per the research questions.

Research Question One

Staff responses to the online Burnout Measure questionnaire related that the mean level of staff burnout was 2.28, with an average standard deviation of 1.22. The

Burnout Measure score of 2.28 falls within the acceptable

range and indicates that staff are at relatively low risk of

job burnout. The results of the burnout measure

questionnaire follow.

Table 5

Descriptive Assessment of Overall Stress

N=20	M	SD
1. How often do you experience: Being Tired?	5.30	0.97
2: How often do you experience: Feeling Depressed?	3.85	1.26
3: How often do you experience: Having a Good Day?	4.50	0.94
4: How often do you experience: Being Physically Exhausted	4.40	1.09
5: How often do you experience: Being Emotionally Exhausted?	4.65	0.98
6: How often do you experience: Being Happy?	4.50	0.88
7: How often do you experience: Being "Wiped Out?"	4.30	0.97
8: How often do you experience: "Can't take it anymore?"	3.65	1.22
9: How often do you experience: Being Unhappy?	4.05	1.09
10: How often do you experience: Feeling Run-Down?	3.95	1.09
11: How often do you experience: Feeling Trapped?	3.90	1.48
12: How often do you experience: Feeling Worthless?	2.65	1.49
13: How often do you experience: Being Weary?	3.30	1.55
14: How often do you experience: Being Troubled?	3.10	1.41
15. How often do you experience: Feeling Disillusioned and Resentful?	3.40	1.78
16: How often do you experience: Being Weak and Susceptible to Illness?	3.15	1.38
17: How often do you experience: Feeling Hopeless?	2.70	1.52

18: How often do you experience: Feeling Rejected?	2.70	1.17
19: How often do you experience: Feeling Optimistic?	4.20	1.15
20: How often do you experience: Feeling Energetic?	3.70	0.97
21: How often do you experience: Feeling Anxious?	4.10	1.25

Research Question Two

The following table shows the actual prevention and intervention strategies as identified by staff during the interviews and focus group.

Table 6

Most Commonly Identified Staff Burnout Prevention and

Intervention Strategies

Intervention and Prevention Strategy	Prevalence of Identification by Staff
Reducing staff-to-client ratios	First most commonly identified
Making downtime available during the workday	Not identified
Limiting hours of stressful work	Not identified
Increasing organizational flexibility	Not identified
Promoting training opportunities	Second most commonly identified
Improving work conditions	Third most commonly identified

Emergent Themes

Reducing Staff-To-Client Ratios

Reducing staff-to-client ratios was identified by all

staff during the interviews and focus group as being an

important strategy for reducing and preventing staff

burnout. Large staff-to-client ratios were reported by

staff to be one of the leading causes of staff burnout due

to a variety of factors, to include the following: (a) not

having enough time to complete work; (b) not being able

to focus properly on the quality of services; (c) not having the time to participate in training; and (d) not having sufficient time to engage in self-care activities. Staff reported that high staff-to-client ratios have a deleterious effect upon most aspects of their job duties.

Making Downtime Available During the Workday

Making downtime available during the workday was not identified as a job burnout prevention or intervention strategy during the interviews or focus group. Conversely, given the commentary by staff regarding the high staff-to-client ratios as well as the high daily workload, making downtime available during the workday may contribute to job stress and burnout. Staff who feel as though they do not have enough time to complete tasks as a normal part of the workday, may experience increased stress if downtime is not part of the workday, and consequently potentiate increased staff burnout.

Limiting Hours of Stressful Work

Limiting hours of stressful work was not identified as a job burnout prevention or intervention strategy during the interviews or focus group. Based upon the information received from the interviews and focus group, it appears to me that work stressors are not caused by work with clients, but rather due to organizational stressors. Limiting hours of stressful work with clients was a factor for alleviating or preventing staff burnout.

Increasing Organizational Flexibility

Increasing organizational flexibility was not identified as a job burnout prevention or intervention strategy during the interviews or focus group. Staff did not report any issues with organizational flexibility. Staff reported working flexible schedules, and that a flexible schedule was a routine part of the workday and part of the position, and that was not identified as a stressor.

Promoting Training Opportunities

All staff identified promoting training opportunities as a method for preventing and alleviating staff burnout. Administrative staff reported the need for additional administrative training, and clinical staff reported the need for additional training regarding client services. Lack of training was identified as a major job stressor because of the fear of performing an incorrect function or job duty, and the reprisal that may be associated with such action due to a lack of knowledge on the part of staff. A general lack of knowledge due to a lack of training was identified as a significant stressor that may lead to job burnout.

Improving Work Conditions

Improving work conditions, as was mentioned in the previous chapter, was loosely defined by Pines and Aronson (1988). Work conditions can be associated with something as benign as a wall color to significant aspect of organizational structure, management, and corporate leadership. Defective work conditions were the most prevalent items that were detailed during the staff interviews and focus group, and encompassed a wide range of issues. Overall themes that were reported by staff during the focus group session and one-on-one interviews included (a) a lack of understanding and engagement of day-to-day operations of offices by upper level management; (b) expectations of staff and managers by upper level management that are incongruent with the actual operations of the offices and office staff; (c) reported lack of interest in learning about the daily operations of offices by upper level management; (d) lack of general as well as specific guidance and support from upper level management; (e) the mission statement is not supported by the organization; (f) lack of appreciation, acknowledgement and recognition for hard work; (g) a generally poor pay scale and no pay raises for staff; (h) broken promises on the part of upper level management; (i) lack of proper staffing levels; (j) poor work environment due to lack of team cohesion or sense of belonging within the organization; and (k) perceived focus on billable services, revenue, and the bottom line profits above all else on the part of upper level management and the organization as a whole.

Implications

The implications from the findings of the study add to the overall body of knowledge pertaining to staff job burnout in the social services, and potential organizational staff burnout prevention and intervention methods. Much of the focus of previous scholarly research has been on the tangible items that organizations can do to prevent or alleviate staff burnout, but less focus has been placed on the role of organizational leadership and structure. I suggest that the implications of the findings of this research may relate that organizational leadership and structure are as important, if not more important than the tangible prevention and intervention strategies that have been suggested in previous scholarly research. I posit that equal attention should be paid to specific organizational burnout prevention and intervention strategies as well as organizational leadership and corporate structure.

Staff burnout appears to be present in most organizations to varying degrees. Corporate leaders should be concerned about burnout and the related denigration of (a) employee morale and productivity, (b) the quality of services rendered or the quality of products produced for clients, and (c) the profitability and efficiency of the organization (Borritz et al., 2006). From an organizational leadership perspective, preventing and alleviating staff burnout through organizational-level methods is crucial (Angermeier et al.,2009). Employees may benefit from high levels of morale and satisfaction in the workplace, thus promoting efficiency and effectiveness. Happy employees might be employees that are more productive. Staff burnout counteracts employee satisfaction and high morale by creating a sense of helplessness, hopelessness, and despair in the workplace (Stalke et al., 2007).

Staff should strive to deliver high-quality goods and services to remain competitive in the marketplace. If an organization's staff suffers from burnout, they might have difficulty maintaining a competitive advantage as the level of product quality and service delivery declines.

This study provides insight for understanding workplace-related stressors that lead to burnout, explores organizational-level coping strategies, and focuses on burnout prevention and intervention strategies that organizational leaders can explore. Organizational staff, leaders, and other stakeholders could benefit from this study because of the potentially positive benefit for the social services agency and its clients.

This case provides organizational leaders with staff burnout prevention and intervention strategies. Ducharme et al. (2008) noted staff burnout within the social services is a serious concern for organizational leaders. Through the identification of staff burnout and understanding organizational prevention and intervention strategies, social services leaders may be able to understand staff burnout more fully. Understanding the significance of staff burnout, in combination with appropriate intervention strategies, might allow organizational leaders to be better equipped to address the issues of staff burnout and to provide more effective organizational-level prevention and intervention

strategies.

Organizational Burnout Prevention and Intervention

Methods- Reconsidered

Pines and Aronson (1988) suggested that the

organizational burnout prevention and interventions that

may be effective for reducing job burnout include (a)

reducing staff-to-client ratios, (b) making downtime

available during the workday, (c) limiting hours of

stressful work, (d) increasing organizational flexibility,

(e) promoting training opportunities, (f) and improving

work conditions. The research suggests that the

development and implementation of the specific and

tangible strategies of reducing staff-to-client ratios and

promoting training opportunities may be the most

important physical strategies that an organization can

employ. Further, the research suggests that the

development and implementation of improving work

conditions through efficacious organizational leadership

and corporate structure may be the most important

psychological aspect for preventing staff job burnout. I

posit that tangible interventions should be targeted and

focused upon the needs of staff and that organizational

leadership and corporate structure should be facilitated in

much the same way to meet the needs of staff and

promote job satisfaction and reduce and prevent job

burnout. The research suggests that these two

intervention and prevention methods should be given

equal priority and attention.

Recommendations for Future Studies

Given that this research addressed the important

topic of staff burnout prevention and intervention

methods, and that organizational leadership and corporate

structure were identified as job stressors more often than

previous research suggests, this study should be

replicated. Future researchers should consider conducting

quasi-experiments from which variables from this study

are used to determine if integration yields reduction in

staff job burnout. Future studies should include both non-profit and for-profit organizations, as well as staff from a wide range of social service organizations.

Researchers should continue working to understand and address specific strategies for preventing and alleviating staff burnout and refrain from implementing or exploring nebulous or difficult to define topics. Likewise, researchers should work to understand the specifics of the organizational leadership and corporate structure and the specific implications for staff regarding job burnout, and ways to prevent and alleviate staff burnout through proposed organizational changes. Future research may be bolstered through long-term studies whereby identified burnout prevention and intervention strategies are implemented for staff within the organization and surveyed for general and specific efficacy.

Summary

In summary, this chapter contains a review of the purpose of the study, discussion of the findings, identification of the themes and emergent themes, ethical considerations of participants, interpretations of the study results, a reconsideration of staff job-burnout prevention and intervention methods. Recommendations for future studies were also addressed. References and Appendices follow accordingly.

REFERENCES

Angermeier, I., Dunford, B. B., Boss, A. D., Boss, R. W. (2009). The impact of participative management perceptions on customer service, medical errors, burnout, and turnover intentions. *Journal of Healthcare Management, 54*(2), 127-141.

Arches, J. (1991). Social structure, burnout, and job satisfaction. *National Association of Social Workers, 36*(3), 202-206.

Ashton, K., Garza, P., & Taylor, B. (2004). Getting down to business: Defining competencies for entry-level youth workers. *Professional Development for Youth Workers: New Directions for Youth Development, 104*, 13-24.

Auerbach, C. F., & Silverstein, L. B. (2003). *Qualitative data: An introduction to coding and analysis.* New York, NY: NYU Press.

Aycock, N., & Boyle, D. (2008). Interventions to manage compassion fatigue in oncology nursing. *Clinical Journal of Oncology Nursing, 13*(2), 183-191.

Bohlander, G., & Snell, S. (2007). *Managing human resources* (14th ed.). Mason, OH: South-Western Cengage.

Borritz, M., Rugulies, R., Bjorner, J. B., Villadsen, E., Mikkelsen, O. A., & Kristensen, T. S. (2006). Burnout among employees in human service work: Design and baseline findings of the PUMA study. *Scandinavian Journal of Public Health, 34*, 49-58.

Bowden, G. (1994). Work stress, burnout and coping: A review and an empirical study of staff in supported housing. *Clinical Psychology and Psychotherapy, 1*(4), 219-232.

Bratton, J., Grint, K., & Nelson, D. L. (2005). *Organizational leadership*. Mason, OH: Thomson South-Western.

Brilliant, E. L. (1986). Social work leadership: A missing ingredient? *Social Work, 31*(5), 325-331.

Brueggemann, W. G. (2006). *The practice of macro social work* (3rd ed.). Belmont, CA: Thomson Higher Education.

Burns, N., & Grove, S.K. (2007). *Understanding nursing research* (4th ed.). St. Louis, MO: Saunders Elsevier.

Busch, M., & Hostetter, C. (2009). Examining organizational learning for application in human service organizations. *Administration in Social Work, 33,* 297-318.

Cherniss, C. (1980). *Staff burnout: Job stress in the human services*. Beverly Hills, CA: Sage.

Cherniss, C., & Egnatios, E. (1978). Is there job satisfaction in community mental health? *Community Mental Health Journal, 14,* 309-318.

Ciulla, J. B. (2003). *The ethics of leadership*. Belmont, CA: Wadsworth/Thomson Learning.

Clark, P. (2009). Resiliency in the practicing marriage and family therapist. *Journal of Marital & Family Therapy, 35*(2), 231-247.

Coffey, M., Dudgill, L., & Tattersall, A. (2004). Stress in social services: Mental well-being, constraints and job satisfaction. *British Journal of Social Work, 34*(5), 735-746.

Coffey, M., Dudgill, L., & Tattersall, A. (2009). Designing a stress management intervention in social services. *International Journal of Workplace Stress Management, 2*(2), 98-114.

Collins, G. (1977). Burn-out: The hazard of professional people helpers. *Christianity Today, 21*, 12-14.

Collins, K., & O'Cathain, A. (2009). Ten points about mixed methods research to be considered by the novice researcher. *International Journal of Multiple Research Approaches, 3*, 2-7.

Cook, T. D.,& Campbell, D. T. (1979). *Quasi-experimentation: Design and analysis for field settings.* Chicago, IL: Rand McNally.

Cooper, D. R., & Schindler, P. S. (2008). *Business research methods.* New York, NY: McGraw-Hill.

Creswell, J. W. (2003). *Research design: Quantitative, qualitative, and mixed methods approaches* (2nd ed.). Thousand Oaks, CA: Sage.

Creswell, J. W. (2009). *Research design: Qualitative, quantitative, and mixed methods approaches* (3rd ed.). Thousand Oaks, CA: Sage.

Creswell, J. W. (2005). *Educational research: Planning, conducting, and evaluating quantitative and qualitative research* (2nd ed.). Upper Saddle River, NJ: Pearson Education.

Creswell, J. W., & Clark, V. L. P. (2007). *Designing and conducting mixed methods research.* Thousand Oaks, CA: Sage.

Creswell, J. W. (2013). *Qualitative inquiry and research design: Choosing among five approaches* (3rd ed.). Thousand Oaks, CA: Sage.

Ciulla, J. B. (2003). *The ethics of leadership*. Belmont, CA: Wadsworth/Thomson Learning.

Daft, R. L. (2008). *The leadership experience* (4th ed.). Mason, OH: Thomson Higher Education.

Daley, M. (1979). "Burnout:" Smoldering problem in protective services. *Social Work, 58*, 375-379.

Denscombe, M. (2007). *The good research guide for small-scale research projects* (3rd ed.). New York, NY: Open University Press.

Deutsch, M., Coleman, P. T., & Marcus, E. C. (Eds.). (2006). *The handbook of conflict resolution: Theory and practice* (2nd ed.). San Francisco, CA: John Wiley & Sons.

Doyle, M., Kelly, D., Clarke, S., & Braynion, P. (2007). Burnout: The impact of psychosocial interventions training. *Mental Health Practice, 10*(7), 16-19.

Drake, B., & Yadama, G. N. (1996). A structural equation model of burnout and job exit among child protective services workers. *Social Work Research, 20*(3), 179-187.

Ducharme, L. J., Knudsen, H. K., & Roman, P. M. (2008). Emotional exhaustion and turnover intention in human service occupations: The protective role of coworker support. *Sociological Spectrum, 28*, 81-104.

Dyer, W. G., Dyer, W. G., & Dyer, J. H. (2007). *Team building: Proven strategies for improving team performance* (4th ed.). San Francisco, CA: Jossey-Bass.

Eastwood, C. D., & Ecklund, K. (2008). Compassion fatigue risk and self-care practices among residential treatment center childcare workers. *Residential Treatment for Children & Youth, 25*(2), 103-122.

Elpers, K., & Westhuis, D. J. (2008). Organizational leadership and its impact on social workers' job satisfaction: A national study. *Administration in Social Work, 32*(3), 26-43.

Evers, J., & van Staa, A., (2009). Qualitative analysis in case study. In *Encyclopedia of case study research*. Retrieved from http://www.sageereference.com.proxy1.ncu.edu/casestudy/Article_n277.html?searchQuery=y%3D0%26quickSearch%3Ddata%2Btriangulation%26x%3D0

Fishkin, G. L. (1994). *American dream, American burnout: How to cope when it all gets to be too much* (1st ed.). Grawn, MI: Loren Publications.

Freeborn, D. K. (2001). Satisfaction, commitment, and psychological well-being among HMO physicians. *Western Journal of Medicine., 174*, 13-18.

Freudenberger, H. (1977). Burn-out: The organizational menace. *Training and Development Journal, 31*, 26-27.

Gall, M., Borg, W., & Gall, J. (2007). *Educational research: An introduction* (8th ed.). Boston, MA: Allyn & Bacon.

Gellis, Z. D., & Kim, J. C. (2004). Predictors of depressive mood, occupational stress, and propensity to leave in older and younger mental health case managers. *Community Mental Health Journal, 40*(5), 407-421.

Glisson, C. (2002). The organizational context of children's mental health services. *Clinical Child & Family Psychology Review, 5*(4), 233-253.

Glisson, C., & Durick, M. (1988). Predictors of Job Satisfaction and Organizational Commitment in Human Service Organizations. *Administrative Science Quarterly, 33*(1), 61-81.

Glisson, C., Schoenwald, S. K., Kelleher, K., Landsverk, J., Eaton-Hoagwood, K., Mayberg, S.,...(2008). Therapist turnover and new program sustainability in mental health clinics as a function of organizational culture, climate, and service structure. *Administration and Policy in Mental Health and Mental Health Services Research, 35*(1), 124-133.

Goetzman, L., Scholz, U., Dux, R., Roelling, M., Boehler, A., Muellhaupth, B.,... Klaghofer, R. (2012). Attitudes towards transplantation and medication among 121 heart, lung, liver and kidney recipients and their spouses. *The European Journal of Medical Sciences: Swiss Medical Weekly,142-153*.

Goethals, G. R., & Sorenson, G. J. L. (Eds.). (2006). *The quest for a general theory of leadership.* Northampton, MA: Edward Elgar.

Graber, J. E., Huang, E. S., Drum, M. L., Chin, M. H., Walters, A. E., Heuer, L.,...(2008). Predicting changes in staff morale and burnout at community health centers participating in the health disparities collaboratives. *Health Research and Educational Trust, 43*(4), 1403-1423.

Grant, A. M., & Campbell, E. M. (2007). Doing good, doing harm, being well and burning out: The interactions and perceived prosocial and antisocial impact in service work. *Journal of Occupational and Organizational Psychology, 80*, 665-691.

Grosch, W. N., & Olsen, D. C. (1994). *When helping starts to hurt : a new look at burnout among psychotherapists* (1st ed.). New York, NY: Norton.

Harrington, D., Bean, N., Pintello, D., & Mathews, D. (2001). Job satisfaction and burnout: Predictors of intentions to leave a job in a military setting. *Administration in Social Work, 25*(3), 1-16.

Hastings, S. (2010). Triangulation. In *Encyclopedia of research design.* Retrieved from http://www.sageereference.com.proxy1.ncu.edu/re searchdesign/Article_n469.html?searchQuery=y% 3D0%26quickSearch%3Ddata%2Btriangulation% 26x%3D0

Hatinen, M., Kinnunen, U., Pekkonen, M., & Kalimo, R. (2007). Comparing two burnout interventions: Perceived job control mediates decreases in burnout. *International Journal of Stress Management, 14*(3), 227-248.

Heifetz, R. A. (1994). *Leadership without easy answers.* Cambridge, MA: Belknap.

Hemmelgarn, A. L., Glisson, C., & James, L. R. (2006). Organizational Culture and Climate: Implications for Services and Interventions Research. *Clinical Psychology: Science and Practice, 13*(1), 73-89.

Hicks, L. (2008). The role of manager in children's homes: The process of managing and leading a well-functioning staff team. *Child and Family Social Work, 13*, 241-251.

Houser, J. (2012). *Nursing research: Reading, using, and creating evidence* (2nd ed.). Sudbury, MA: Jones & Bartlett Learning.

Huxley, P., Evans, S., Gately, C., Webber, M., Mears, A., Pajak, S.,...(2005). Stress and pressures in mentla health social work: The worker speaks. *British Journal of Social Work, 2005*(7), 1063-1079.

Jaffe, D. T., & Scott, C., D. (1984). *From burnout to balance*. New York, NY: McGraw-Hill.

Jansson, B. S. (2009). *The reluctant welfare state: Engaging history to advance social work practice in contemporary society* (6th ed.). Belmont, CA: Brooks/Cole.

Kao, Y. (2009). Burnout in college student volunteers: A cross-level study. *College Student Journal, 43*(3), 872-878.

Katzenbach, J. R., & Smith, D. K. (1993). *The wisdom of teams: Creating the high-performance organization*. Boston, MA: Harvard Business School Press.

Kirst-Ashman, K. K., & Hull, G. H. (2009). *Understanding generalist practice* (5th ed.). Belmont, CA: Brooks/Cole.

Koeske, G. F., & Koeske, R. D. (1989). Work Load and Burnout: Can Social Support and Perceived Accomplishment Help? [Article]. *Social Work, 34*(3), 243-248.

Koeske, G. F., & Kirk, S. A. (1993). Coping with job stress: Which strategies work best? *Journal of Occupational & Organizational Psychology, 66*(4), 319-335.

Kompier, M. A. J., Cooper, C. L., & Geurts, S. A. E. (2000). A multiple case study approach to work stress prevention in Europe. *European Journal of Work & Organizational Psychology, 9*(3), 371-400.

Kotter, J. P., & Cohen, D. S. (2002). *The heart of change: Real life stories of how people change their organizations.* Boston, MA: Harvard Business School Publishing.

Krippendorff, K. (2004). *Content analysis, an introduction to its methodology* (2nd ed.). Thousand Oaks, CA: Sage.

Lee, S. M., Cho, S. H., Kissinger, D., & Ogle, N. T. (2010). A typology of burnout in professional counselors. *Journal of Counseling and Development, Spring 2010*(88), 131-138.

Leedy, P., & Ormrod, J. (2010). *Practical research: Planning and design* (9th ed.). Upper Saddle River, NJ: Prentice-Hall.

Leiter, M. P., & Maslach, C. (2005). *Banishing burnout: Six strategies for improving your relationship with work.* San Francisco, CA: John Wiley & Sons.

Lewandowski, C. A. (2003). Organizational factors contributing to worker frustration: The precursor to burnout. *Journal of Sociology and Social Welfare, XXX*(4), 175-185.

Leyba, E. G. (2009). Tools to reduce overload in the school social worker role. *National Association of Social Workers, 31*(4), 219-228.

Lincoln, Y.S., & Guba, E.G. (1985). *Naturalistic inquiry.* Beverly Hills, CA: Sage.

Liossis, P. L., Shochet, I. M., Millear, P. M., & Biggs, H. (2009). The promoting adult resilience (PAR) program: The effectiveness of the second, shorter pilot of a workplace prevention program. *Behaviour Change, 26*(2), 97-112.

Mancini, M. A., & Lawson, H. A. (2009). Facilitating positive emotional labor in peer-providers of mental health services. *Administration in Social Work, 33*(1), 3-22.

Maslach, C. (1976) Burned out. *Human Behavior, 5*, 16-22.

Maslach, C. (2003). *Burnout: The cost of caring.* Cambridge, MA: Malor Books.

Maslach, C., Jackson, S.E., & Leitner, M.P. (1996). *The Maslach burnout inventory: Manual* (3rd ed.). Palo Alto, CA. Consulting Psychologist Press.

Maslach, C., & Leiter, M. P. (2008). Early predictors of job burnout and engagement. *Journal of Applied Psychology, 93*(3), 498-512.

Maslach, C., Schaufeli, W.B., & Leiter, M.P. (2001). Job burnout. *Annual Review of Psychology, 52*, 397-422.

Maslow, A. H. (1948). Some theoretical consequences of basic need-gratification. *Journal of Personality, 16*(4), 402-416.

Mendel, W. (1979). Staff burn-out: Diagnosis, treatment, and prevention. *New Directions in Mental Health Services, 2*, 75-83.

Miles, M., & Huberman, A. (1994). *Qualitative data analysis: An expanded sourcebook.* Thousand Oaks, CA: Sage.

Morse, J., & Richards, L. (2002). *Read me first for a user's guide to qualitative methods.* Thousand Oaks, CA: Sage.

Mostert, K., & Joubert, A. F. (2005). Job stress, burnout and coping strategies in the South African police service. *South African Journal of Economic and Management* Sciences, *8*(1), 39-53.

Munn-Giddings, C., Hart, C., & Ramon, S. (2005). A participatory approach to the promotion of well-being in the workplace: Lessons from empirical research. *International Review of Psychiatry, 17*(5), 409-417.

Munro, J. H. (Ed.). (2008). *Organizational leadership.* Dubuque, IA: McGraw-Hill.

Newman, M. A., Guy, M. E., & Mastracci, S. H. (2009). Beyond cognition: Affective leadership and emotional labor. *Public Administration Review, 69*(1), 6-20.

Newton, L. H., & Ford, M. M. (Eds.). (2006). *Taking sides: Clashing views in business ethics and society* (9th ed.). Dubuque, IA.: McGraw-Hill.

Ngai, S. S., & Cheung, C. (2009). Idealism, altruism, career orientation, and emotional exhaustion among social work undergraduates. *Journal of Social Work Education, 45*(1), 105-121.

Northouse, P. G. (2007). *Leadership: Theory and practice* (4th ed.). Thousand Oaks, CA: Sage Publications.

Nurmi, J., Salmela-Aro, K. K. P., & Naatanen, P. (2008). Confidence in work-related goals and feelings of exhaustion during a therapeutic intervention for burnout: A time-series approach. *Journal of Occupational and Organizational Psychology, 81*(2), 277-297.

O'Donnell, J., & Kirkner, S. L. (2009). A longitudinal study of factors influencing the retention of Title IV-E master's of social work graduates in public child welfare. *Journal of Public Child Welfare, 3*(1), 64-86.

Oginska-Bulik, N. (2006). Occupational stress and its consequences in health care professions: The role of type D personality. *International Journal of Occupational Medicine and Environmental Health, 19*(2), 113-122.

Pasupuleti, S., Allen, R. I., Lambert, E. G., & Cluse-Tolar, T. (2009). The impact of work stressors on the life satisfaction of social service workers: A preliminary study. *Administration in Social Work, 33*(3), 319-339.

Patton, M. (1990). *Qualitative evaluation and research methods*. London, England, UK: Sage.

Pedhazur, E. J., & Schmelkin, L. P. (1991). *Measurement, design, and analysis: An integrated approach.* Hillsdale, NJ: Erlbaum.

Pedrini, L., Magni, L. R., Giovannini, C., Panetta, V., Zacchi, V., Rossi, G.,...(2009). Burnout in nonhospital psychiatric residential facilities. *Psychiatric Services, 60*(11), 1547-1551.

Peterson, U., Bergstrom, G., Samuelsson, M., Asberg, M., & Nygren, A. (2008). Reflecting peer-support groups in the prevention of stress and burnout: Randomized controlled trial. *Journal of Advanced Nursing, 63*(5), 506-516.

Peterson, U., Demerouti, E., Bergstrom, G., Asberg, M., & Nygren, A. (2008). Work characteristics and sickness absence in burnout and non-burnout groups: A study of Swedish health care workers. *International Journal of Stress Management, 15*(2), 153-172.

Pines, A. M. (2000). Nurses' burnout: An existential psychodynamic perspective. *Journal of Psychosocial Nursing, 38*(2), 1-9.

Pines, A. M., & Aronson, E. (1988). *Career burnout.* New York, NY: The Free Press.

Pines, A., & Maslach, C. (1978). Characteristics of staff burn-out in mental health settings. *Hospital Community Psychiatry, 29*, 233-237.

Polkinghome, D. E. (2005). Language and meaning: Data collection in qualitative research. *Journal of Counseling Psychology, 52* (2), 137-145.

Potter, B. A. (1996). *Preventing job burnout: Transforming work pressures into productivity* (Revised ed.). Menlo Park, CA: Crisp Learning.

Powell, K. (1993). *Burnout: What happens when stress gets out of control and how to regain your sanity.* London, England, UK: Thorsons.

Rank, M. G., & Hutchison, W. S. (2000). An analysis of leadership within the social work profession. *Journal of Social Work Education, 36*(3), 487-502.

Raquepaw, J. M., & Miller, R. S. (1989). Psychotherapist burnout: A componential analysis. *Professional Psychology: Research and Practice, 20*(1), 32-36.

Rossman, G. B., & Wilson, B. L. (1985). Numbers and words: Combining, quantitative, and qualitative methods in a single large-scale evaluation study. *Evaluation Review, 9*, 627-643.

Rothmann, S., Jackson, L. T. B., & Kruger, M. M. (2003). Burnout and job stress in a local government: The moderating effect of sense of coherence. *South African Journal of Industrial Psychology, 29*(4), 52-60.

Rycraft, J. R. (1994). The party isn't over: The agency role in the retention of public child welfare caseworkers. *Social Work, 39*(1), 75-80.

Sadovich, J. (2006). Work excitement in nursing: An examination of the relationship between work excitement and burnout. *Nursing Economics, 23*, 91-96.

Salmela-Aro, K., Naatanen, P., & Nurmi, J. (2004). The role of work-related personal projects during two burnout interventions: A longitudinal study. *Work & Stress, 18*(3), 208-230.

Sandmark, H., & Renstig, M. (2010). Understanding long-term sick leave in female white-collar workers with burnout and stress related diagnoses: A qualitative study. *BioMed Central Public Health, 10*(210), 1-12.

Schaer, M., Bodenmann, G., & Klink, T. (2008). Balancing work and relationships: Couples coping enhancement training (CCET) in the workplace. *Applied Psychology: An International Review, 57*(1), 71-89.

Schaufeli, W. B., & Enzmann, D. (1998). *The burnout companion to study and practice: A critical analysis*. London, England, UK: Taylor & Francis.

Schaufeli, W. B., Maslach, C., & Marek, T. (Eds.). (1993). *Professional burnout: Recent developments in theory and research*. New York, NY: Taylor & Francis.

Schaufeli, W. B., Taris, T. W., & van Rhenen, W. (2007). Workaholism, burnout, and work engagement: Three of a kind or three different kinds of employee well-being? *Applied Psychology: An International Review, 57*(2), 173-203.

Schulz, R., Greenley, J. R., & Brown, R. (1995). Organization, management, and client effects on staff burnout. *Journal of Health and Social Behavior, 36*(3), 333-345.

Schwartz, R. H., Tiamiyu, M. F., & Dwyer, D. J. (2007). Social worker hope and perceived burnout: The effects of age, years in practice, and setting. *Administration in Social Work, 31*(4), 103-119.

Shenton, A. K. (2004). Strategies for ensuring trustworthiness in qualitative research projects. *Education for Information, 22*, 63-75.

Shockley-Zalabak, P. S. (2009). *Fundamentals of organizational communication: Knowledge, sensitivity, skills, values*. Boston, MA: Allyn & Bacon.

Siebert, D. C. (2005). Personal and occupational factors in burnout among practicing social workers: Implications for researchers, practitioners, and managers. *Journal of Social Service Research, 32*(2), 25-44.

Simendinger, E. A., & Moore, T. F. (1985). *Organizational burnout in health care facilities: Strategies for prevention and change*. Rockville, MD: Aspen Systems Corp.

Stalker, C. A., Mandell, D., Frensch, K. M., Harvey, C., & Wright, M. (2007). Child welfare workers who are exhausted yet satisfied with their jobs: How do they do it? *Child and Family Social Work, 12*(2), 182-191.

Storey, J., & Billingham, J. (2001). Occupational stress and social work. *Social Work Education, 20*(6), 659-670.

Strauss, A., & Corbin, J. (Eds.) (1990). *Basics of qualitative research: Ground theory procedures and techniques*. Newbury Park, CA: Sage.

Strolin-Goltzman, J., Kollar, S., & Trinkle, J. (2010). Listening to the voices of children in foster care: Youths speak out about child welfare workforce turnover and selection. *Social Work, 55*(1), 47-53.

Studies, C. F. H. W. (2006). *Licensed social workers in the United States*. Washington, DC: The National Association of Social Workers Center for Workforce Studies.

Taris, T. W., Kompier, M. A. J., Geurts, S. A. E., Schreurs, P. J. G., Schaufeli, W. B., de Boer, E.,...(2003). Stress Management Interventions in the Dutch Domiciliary Care Sector: Findings From 81 Organizations. *International Journal of Stress Management, 10*(4), 297-325.

Tashakkori, A., & Teddie, C. (1998). *Mixed methodology: Combining qualitative and quantitative approaches*. Thousand Oaks, CA: Sage.

Teddie, C., & Tashakkori, A. (2009). *Foundations of mixed methods research*. Thousand Oaks, CA: Sage.

Thurmond, V. (2001). The point of triangulation. *Journal of Nursing Scholarship, 33*(3), 254-256.

Van Hook, M. P., & Rothenberg, M. (2009). Quality of life and compassion satisfaction/fatigue and burnout in child welfare workers: A study of the child welfare workers in community based care organizations in central Florida. *Social Work & Christianity, 36*(1), 36-54.

Wilkerson, K. (2009). An examination of burnout among school counselors guided by stress-strain-coping theory. *Journal of Counseling & Development, 87*(4), 428-437.

Williams, E.S., & Skinner, A.C. (2003). Outcomes of physician job satisfaction: A narrative review, implications, and directions for future research. *Health Care Management Review. 28*, 119-139

Wolfe, G. (1981). Burnout of therapists: Inevitable or preventable? *Journal of the American Physical Therapy Association, 61*, 1046-1050.

Xanthakis, A. (2009). Levels of work-stress and burnout among prison officers: An examination of the need for a staff counseling service in a forensic setting. *Counseling Psychology Review, 24*(3/4), 100-118.

Yin, R. K. (2009). *Case study research: Design and methods* (4th ed.). Thousand Oaks, CA: Sage.

Yu, M., Lin, C., & Hsu, S. (2009). Stressors and burnout: The role of employee assistance programs and self-efficacy. *Social Behavior and Personality, 37*(3), 365-377.

Zastrow, C. H., & Kirst-Ashman, K. K. (2010). *Understanding human behavior and the social environment* (8th ed.). Belmont, CA: Brooks/Cole.

APPENDIX A

Burnout Measure Self-Assessment

You can compute your burnout score by completing the
following questionnaire.
How often do you have any of the following experiences?
Please use the scale:

1	2	3	4	5	6	7
Never	Once in a great while	Rarely	Sometimes	Often	Usually	Always

_____	1. Being tired.
_____	2. Feeling depressed.
_____	3. Having a good day.
_____	4. Being physically exhausted.
_____	5. Being emotionally exhausted.
_____	6. Being happy.
_____	7. Being "wiped out."
_____	8. "Can't take it anymore."
_____	9. Being unhappy.
_____	10. Feeling run-down.
_____	11. Feeling trapped.
_____	12. Feeling worthless.
_____	13. Being weary.
_____	14. Being troubled.
_____	15. Feeling disillusioned and resentful.
_____	16. Being weak and susceptible to illness.
_____	17. Feeling hopeless
_____	18. Feeling rejected.
_____	19. Feeling optimistic.
_____	20. Feeling energetic.
_____	21. Feeling anxious.

Computation of score:

Add the values you wrote next to the following items:

1, 2, 4, 5, 7, 8, 9, 10, 11, 12, 13, 14, 15, 16, 17, 18, 21 (A) _____.

Add the values you wrote next to the following items: 3, 6, 19, 20 (B) _____, subtract (B) from 32 (C) _____.

Add A and C (D) _____.

Divide D by 21_____. This is your burnout score.

APPENDIX B

Individual Interview Questions

1. Bearing in mind the six organizational coping strategies for reducing and preventing staff burnout as described by Pines and Aronson (1988) to include (a) reducing staff-to-client ratios, (b) making downtime available during the workday, (c) limiting hours of stressful work, (d) increasing organizational flexibility, (e) promoting training opportunities, (f) and improving work conditions, which strategy or strategies do you believe would be the most beneficial for staff at this agency?

2. Why do you believe that specific strategy will be effective for reducing and preventing staff burnout?

    2.1 How did you come to that point of view?

3. What burnout prevention and intervention strategy or strategies do you believe would be beneficial for staff at this agency that are not included in this list?

    3.1 How did you come to that point of view?

4. What factors of factors do you believe contribute to staff burnout at this agency that we have not already discussed?

    4.1 Why do you believe that to be true?

APPENDIX C

Group Interview Questions

1. Bearing in mind the six organizational coping strategies for reducing and preventing staff burnout as described by Pines and Aronson (1988) to include (a) reducing staff-to-client ratios, (b) making downtime available during the workday, (c) limiting hours of stressful work, (d) increasing organizational flexibility, (e) promoting training opportunities, (f) and improving work conditions, which strategy or strategies do you believe would be the most beneficial for staff at this agency?

2. Why do you believe that specific strategy will be effective for reducing and preventing staff burnout?

3. What burnout prevention and intervention strategy or strategies do you believe would be beneficial for staff at this agency that are not included in this list?

4. What factors of factors do you believe contribute to staff burnout at this agency that we have not already discussed?

EPILOGUE

While this case study is limited in scope, it is my hope that it will inspire others to conduct further research on the topic of staff burnout in the social services professions. The field of social services as a whole is slated to increase dramatically in the coming years as more of an emphasis is placed upon proactively preventing disease and illness rather than reacting to such issues after they have taken root. This increased demand for and upon professionals will undoubtedly strain an already over worked, under-recruited, underdeveloped, and historically underfunded workforce.

During the literature review phase of the project I found it surprisingly difficult to locate major studies and seminal works related to staff burnout in the social services in the United States. Studies have been conducted, but many were not as recent as I had hoped for. Moreover, many of the recent studies were conducted in foreign countries in what many Americans refer to with disdain as Socialized Medicine. The foreign studies placed great emphasis on employee job satisfaction and improving patient outcomes, and how the two are intertwined. There was little or no mention of the costs associated with these factors as they were non-optional and viewed as an integral aspect of quality healthcare. This was a significant and reoccurring theme that stood out as a topic that deserves serious scholarly investigation.

One should explore if the focus on profit in our privatized medical model leaves *less* room for an emphasis on decreasing staff burnout and improving patient/client outcomes as corporations seek to bolster the bottom line and please shareholders. Decreasing staff burnout and improving job satisfaction have been related to improved patient/client outcomes, and positive outcomes should always be our primary objective. In the grand scheme of things, when professionals seek to help fellow humans through the myriad of physical and emotional issues they may face, should not shareholders be last on the list of priorities? Should shareholders in for-profit healthcare corporations invest in such institutions from more of an altruistic perspective versus the expectation of a solid return on investment? If not, we may need to explore whether or not for-profit healthcare corporations should exist within our healthcare systems in the Unites States. A study of the differences and similarities between non-profit and for-profit healthcare corporations as related to employee burnout, job satisfaction and outcomes may also prove beneficial.

It is my hope that the information presented in this study will help current researchers and researchers to be, and spur further discourse on this important topic.

Best regards,

Robert C. Cowan, Ed.D.

www.ingramcontent.com/pod-product-compliance
Lightning Source LLC
Chambersburg PA
CBHW060248290526
45789CB00001B/245